# THE LIFE OF BRI

## FOREVER YOUNG

### BY

### BRIAN HAMBLETT

# CONTENT

Many thanks to all the great people that coloured my world in the late sixties and early seventies, and of course Stew who created these memories with me all those years ago.

For my friends and fantastic family, especially my wonderful father that left us just before Christmas, 2013.

You are never far from our thoughts and only ever a dream away.

'The Diggy'
Moston

## PLAY IT AGAIN, STEW

My mother had been quietly reading the News of the World, Radio 2 was on in the background, her pink slippered feet were raised and resting on the settee when her Sunday post cleaning wind-down came to a loud, abrupt halt as the front door crashed open and I, like Billy Whizz, raced through the living room. I was halfway to the kitchen when she called me back.

"Hey, you noisy little devil, what's the rush? Do you need the toilet?" she asked angrily.

"Er, no mam, me, Stew and Trumper have been on the Tip... And we've found loads of treasure!" my excited voice rising to almost a falsetto, my eyes on fire with excitement.

"Whoa, hold on, what sort of treasure? It's not another car tyre is it?" trepidation dripping from her words.

"Nooooo... Miles better," I stopped and thought of my 'hoop' and stick... " heeyyy, by the way, where is that? I've not seen it in ages!"

"Forget it, Bri, it's long gone... Car tyres are not toys! I hope it's not another shop dummy is it?, You scared the living daylights out of me when you threw it over the gate... There's me, washing the pots, looking through the kitchen window... And then I suddenly thought a naked man had leapt into the yard!!" the memory causing her right eye to twitch.

"Do you mean me giant Action Man? Where's that too? Hey, all of me old treasure's missing!"

9

"Shush now… Just tell me what you think you're bringing into the back yard."

"You're not gonna believe it mum… Someone's actually thrown this away!"

"Thrown what away?" she was getting irritated now.

"It's a musical instrument. You like 'em too!" I started edging my way to the kitchen.

"Which musical instrument? It's not a trombone is it? You've not put your lips on it, have you?

"No… What's a trumpbone… Is that something a dog eats?"

"No, it's like a trumpet… " she looked at my eye's beginning to glaze over and stopped, "… It doesn't matter, just tell me what have you got out there."

"It's one of them things that that fat woman played on Morecambe and Wise, the other night."

Mum's eye's raised up and to the left as she ran through the episode we had watched two nights previously.

"Fat woman… Mrs Mills? It's not a piano is it? Brian, it's not a piano?"

"That's it, couldn't think of the name, cost I'm so excited, a real pianna… A real one… With nearly all the keys!" shaking my head at the unbelievable luck I had in finding it.

"Oh no you don't, sunny Jim… " she tried to get passed me.

"Whaaat… It's a real pianna… It works an everything… I'll be able to learn how to play it and we can all sing things like Lily the Pink, it'll be brill… Come and look, Stew's at the back gate." I moved slowly towards the back door… My eye's imploring mum to just look, allow herself to fall in love, like I had, with the wonderful wooden musical upright.

"I am not having a piano in this house, there's no room, and it's off the bloody tip!!!" her arms folded very tightly as if to back up her words.

"Come on, just look... " I unlatched the kitchen door and pulled it open, and immediately a cacophony of noise washed over us from just beyond our back gate, it was the sound of a piano being viciously attacked, unmercifully... And each and every key was being bashed in non-melodic dyslexia.

"Good God!" mum pushed me gently to one side and in three large strides she was across the yard and opening the back gate... And there, Stewart was banging... And I mean literally banging on the keys on an old upright piano, the biggest, happiest smile painted on his face.

"Wow Stew, that sounds great" I said to him as I popped my head under my mother's arm that held the gate open...

"No, no... It sounds... Oh my God. Stewart, Stewart dear, stop the banging, please." all along the back bedroom windows of Levens Street, curtain were pulled aside for a better view. Some heads popping round the gates in the ginnel, all wide eyed, all slack jawed, all causing my mum's heart to beat faster, really not wanting all this attention.

"Do you like it, Marie?" Stew had stopped the musical outrage but still had that enormous grin, like this was a gift from God.

"Stewart, you really need to take it back to the tip, we haven't got room for a piano here."

Confusion appeared on his face.

"But it's a piano!"

"I know, I've told her, Stew."

"Why not take it to your house then?" mum ignored my interruption as she spoke to Stew.

"My mum and dad would kill me... They don't like me bringing fings home." his head slumped in remembrance of all the things he'd had ejected from his premises.

Mum's head started shaking, while Trumper squeezed between Stew's legs, sniffing at the base of the upright, a small

11

growl coming from deep in his throat. He started walking round, like he was following something inside.

"What's wrong with your dog, Brian?" mum asked.

"Don't know mum, can I keep the piano... Mum, can I, can I?"

"No, Brian, and that's my final answer!" as she spoke she followed Trumper as he got more excited. "Brian, why is Trumper growling?" there was a worried tone in her voice now.

Stew climbed up, knees on the keyboard, causing another loud mish mash of sound that made my mother wince. He carefully lifted the narrow, dark wooden lid and peered inside, Trumper was barking now, getting very excited.

"Oooh... I fink there's a mouse in here, Hammy, oooh... And it's a big one too. It's got... " Stew looked round when he heard the back gate crash shut, my mother's scream cutting through his sentence like a scalpel. "... A really, really long tail!" his voice trailing off quietly as he realised he was all alone.

Then, my head appeared over the gate, it had an unhappy face on it.

"Mum says if it's not out of the entry in the next two minutes, she's gonna leave home, annnnd, she says that sounds like a rat!"

"How does your mum know what a rat sounds like?" he inquired.

"I don't know... But we're going to have to push it back, although, we could take it to our den, we can try and learn a song, and then when we have we can show her how good we are. She'll want a piano in the yard then... She'll wonder why she ever said no... And when we get on Opportunity Knocks and get famous she'll have to apologise" I said this as I struggled over the gate.

"Yeah, we can get that broken telly we saw. Smash the glass and we can put our faces through the back... Pretend we're on the box... And practise for Opportunity Knocks... "

"Ooooh, yeah, and we could pretend we are Garrison's Gorillas... "

"Bag's I'm Chief!" Stew said quickly.

"Awww, flippin eck... Okay... Bags I'm Garrison then... I like Chief with his flick knives... " disappointment in my voice.

"Right, let's push this back... Do you think I can keep the mouse as a pet, train it to do tricks?" Stew asked.

"Yeah, why not? You could teach it to follow you, you'd look like the Pied Piper... Get a recorder from school... Hey, that would look good on Opportunity Knocks! If a man flexing his muscles can win... A boy making a mouse dance with a recorder is a shoe in!"

"What if I did that and you played the pianna... The Pied Piper and Hamblett... What a name! Perfect... Hughie Green will wet himself when he sees us!"

All this dreaming helped with the pushing, Trumper continued with his aggressive attitude towards the instrument.

"You're gonna have to teach the Trumpster to be more friendly, you know, he's really got 'em on him today!"

"Trumper... Cheer up matey, when we get Stew's new pet out... You can play with him then." I tried to placate him.

Two young boy's, both bent at 45 degrees as they pushed the upright piano up Rudd Street towards the tip in the distance, a shabby looking mutt walking at the side of the piano, letting the rodent inside know he wanted to play, and a mother, hands on chest, eyes closed with her back against a latched and bolted back door...

"Those bloody boys... They're driving me up the wall."

13

## WAITING ON LOVE

Up to the age of 11, at the end of each school day, I would head home from Lily Lane junior school. I would walk out through the big iron gate on Lizmar Terrace and cross over Lily Lane itself and on to McConnell Road. By this time, I would have been joined by Steve Miller, Alan Moore and Stuart McGovern, all would have our hands pushed deep into our shorts. We would be talking and laughing about football, Slade or T Rex as we made our way on to the Diggy behind The Sharon Church, homeward bound.

The Diggy, was large expanse of flat dirt, the surface was how I imagined the Moon's surface to be, like crushed coal. It had a set of goalposts at the start and another set at the end. On our left were dozens of barely standing garages, behind the furthest goalposts was even more garages, bigger, but no more impressive. This grim landscape was a big part of my young life's playground.

On our immediate right was the swing park... And if the weather permitted we may take a slide or a manic, life threatening, spin on the roundabout on our route home... But eventually we would cross the pitch and that black-grey cinder surface. Dust would be coming up with each and every step, slowly colouring our legs, when our socks came off later it would have left us with the Diggy tan, very white feet where the dust hadn't penetrated and mucky grey on our exposed legs...

The Tip bordered the 'swingy,' and was pure desolation. It was behind a rudimentary two-bar rusting metal fence and was also on the right, a small boundary path ran between where it began and where the park ended. It was home to burnt out cars... Smashed tv's... Basically anything that anyone didn't want dropped it over the fence, either by hand or from the back of a car, it was also home to lots of rats. It went off to the horizon towards Church Lane and Moston Brook. The tip was a haven for young lads... One man's rubbish was another boy's treasure!

We walked on, I would have almost certainly kicked a stone the full length of the pitch and attempted to score in through the goalposts before running back into line with my pals and taking the slight rise, past Billy Owens garage towards Rudd Street. Billy was our rag and bone man, he always locked his alsatian in the garage to protect his stock and each time we passed it would go bonkers through the gap in the double-gated door, especially if you stuck a stick through to antagonise him. Poor thing was the only fatality when it was burnt to the ground a few years later.

And that was the Diggy, in my young boys head it was a massive acreage of dirt and fun, in truth it was only probably a few hundred yards from start to finish and the same across, from the backs of houses on Brendon Avenue over to the swingy and the Tip.

As the Diggy finished, Rudd Street began, and Alan's house was two doors in. Alan would open his door and his barmy dog, a big yellow over friendly beast, would bound out, leaping on anyone close by, and for some strange reason he took a fancy to me in particular. He would lock his front paws on me and bonk my leg passionately. My screams causing my friends to laugh and cheer. I would try to escape... No matter how fast I ran, and God, did I run, and he would follow.

Once Alan had eventually controlled his horny hound, we would continue home,

15

Miller would bid farewell seconds later as he exited left, up Levens Street, Then Stu crossed over to go down his street. Alone I would go up the ginnel between Lakin Street and Levens. Mine was the second gate in, it was locked and so I would climb.

It would take lots of leg scrambling until I sat atop it, a leg either side of the gate. There I would take a breather, then I clamber down, sometimes fall, like a sack of coal into our backyard.

Once safely back on terra firma I would cross to our whitewashed toilet on the right, creak the flimsy door open and sit, lid down of course... Prop my feet up on the open door. In my hand would be the Beezer or Dandy, put in there by my mum so I would be entertained for the 45 minutes or so until her return. I would read, giggle and dream until she came home from her days work.

Then, around 4.05, mum would be done at Charlie's the corner shop, it was adjacent to Leeming's and next to Dave's newsagents on Lightbowne Road... And if I close my eyes, I can still hear the latch lift... And then the bolt slide open on our kitchen back door now... The green door would open and my Mum's lovely face and smile would suddenly light up the doorframe. And in I would run... Straight into biggest and best hugs in Moston. Into her arms, into our home.

All this should be filmed in grainy, black and white, with the Brighouse and Rastrick Brass Band playing Concierto de Aranjuez very softly in the background. Slow motion shots of me kicking a large stone through the top nets, my mop top hair straggly and unkempt, as the 'ball' flies through the posts my arms raise stiffly by my cheeks, skyward, with my head thrown back and a full beam smile ala Georgie Best. You see, that was me, a child of the sixties... Just a happy, pudgy, Moston boy.

## A MEAL AND THE DETECTIVES

It had been raining and the wet, grey pavement slabs reflected the yellow street lamps on Kenyon Lane, lighting the way. Mum and Dad were going out to celebrate their 10th wedding anniversary and I was tagging along, not because they wanted me with them, but the babysitter had bailed on them half an hour before she was due.

"You'd better behave in here." mum said sternly, looking down at me. "... And hold my hand, will you?" she really wasn't hiding her disappointment very well.

"I'm not holding your hand on a pavement, there's no point, there's no cars on the pavement, and if there was, holding your hand wouldn't save me, would it? In fact, holding your hand might just stop me from being able to leap to safety... I don't mind holding it when we cross any roads, but not just walking on a pavement. I'm not a baby." I looked up at her, she was not happy. "I've never been in a proper restaurant, have I?" changing the subject quickly.

"And if you don't behave... You never will again!" mum said.

"Well, you can't stop me going in one when I'm 21, I'll be a man... I can do..."I stopped as I looked at her, and turned to my dad in front..."What you gonna have, dad?"

Dad, who was using his long legs to stay just ahead, was in his dark blue suit, crisp white shirt and a thin navy tie that finished the look off perfectly. Tall, lean and handsome with a permanent grin affixed to his face, here was a man happy with his lot. He turned his head and told me he was going to have the biggest, thickest steak on the menu.

"I might do as well... "

"No you bloody won't... Burger and chips for you. Like it or lump it... Steak!! Pfft" the idea of wasting hard earned money on sirloin steak for a child in primary school was a ludicrous thought.

"Burger... Can I have a cheeseburger then... ?"!

"Wait until we get in there, we'll see what's available." he had turned away again to look where he was going.

"Hey dad, that's my school!" Lily Lane primary had popped into view ahead of us on the left. "Whoa... The lights are on! Is that what night school is?"

"No, its teachers fight night, son! Your headmaster is fighting your teacher tonight in the sports hall." Dad said rather convincingly.

"No way... Mr Beckett is fighting Mr Roney! He'll marmalize him. Mr Roney's about 80 year's old." then I imagined them in leotards and grinned.

"Don't listen to your father, Brian, he's talking nonsense again." mum interrupted.

I looked at dad and he pursed his lips and gave a slight nod confirming he was indeed telling the truth. I stared at the school as we walked by, dreaming that my Mr Roney had Beckett in a Boston Crab hold, and was ignoring his screams to be released.

"Mr Beckett hates me."

"I wonder if that has anything to do with your mouth?" mum asked.

"I don't think so... Nowt wrong with my gob" I touched my lips as I said this.

"It was a rhetorical question, Brian." mum tutted.

"A regorical question... What's that?" I asked, bemused.

"Rhetorical. It's a question that doesn't require an answer!"

"Then it's not a question, is it?" a confused look spread slowly across my face.

"Yes. It is a question... Erm... It's one that has such an obvious answer that you don't need to answer it."

"Well if you're asking a question you know the answer too, what's the point in asking the question? Seems like a waste of words... Hey dad?" I tried to involve my father who was still whistling quietly in isolation.

"Now, don't get me involved... Just agree with your mum...
"

"And, what's that supposed to mean? Just agree with your mother just for a bit of peace?" she called after my dad.

He lifted both arms in apparent surrender... Then explained that a son should not be arguing with his mother, especially on her wedding anniversary.

"Right... Well... Yes... Listen to your father, Brian." she stammered in doubt of dad's sincerity.

"You told me not to listen to him before, when he said my teachers were going to be boxing tonight!" I was getting confused. "Do I listen to him or not?"

"This is you... " she said to my dad, pointing at his back, her voice quiet but stern, "... Way too much sarcasm... Joking about everything, no wonder his head is in the clouds."

Dad just apologised quietly, he kept up his stride and began his whistle again after  suggesting we cross over, The Galleon restaurant was not far away but it was located on the other side of Kenyon Lane.

"Here son, get hold of my hand, now look both ways...okay, walk quickly... Don't run. I've got heels on, stay at my side... Do not kick that stone... No... Big Brian, will you have a word with your son... ?" mum ordered as we tried to cross.

"Do as your mum says… " dad shouted without looking back.

"Okay dad." I agreed all too quickly.

"Is that it… ?" mum railed at dad, "… Do as your mum says… ?"

"What do you want me to say?"

"Tell him to behave… Or… He's in trouble, showing me up… And, look at his shoe now."

"Behave… Or else… " he had stopped and waited for me, he had changed his tone and although he had never hit me… but I was not going to push my luck… I had seen his hands, the size of tennis rackets, and I suspected his forearm smash would be a winner.

"Sorry dad… "

"Not to me… To your mother." he pointed to my mum, who seemed happier angry dad had finally turned up.

"Sorry mum. I'll behave… Honest injun." I walked slowly beside her with my best hangdog expression.

"Well, that's okay, no more kicking stones and when we get in the restaurant, be polite at the table." she mussed my hair to show she still loved me… Even if she didn't trust me.

Two minutes later dad pushed open the door, recently varnished in a cherry wood colour, the top half segmented by six small sections of glass. All different autumnal colours, yellow, red and orange. The two main front bow windows where larger versions of the door, I think it was supposed to be like the stern of a galleon ship… A galleon designed by a gay pirate, that is.

"Good evening sir, madam, and err… Boy" the waiter was obviously not taken by the sight of me, white shirt half in and half out of my trousers. As he looked on my mum bowed down to start attempting to tuck it back in, under my waistline. I moaned and groaned, twisted and insisted I could do it myself.

"Table for Hamblett, please, we have booked." dad said.

"Table for two!" the man said as he looked in a ledger that was sat on what looked like a small lectern. He gripped both sides of the wooden stand, but refused to look up at my dad. Dad towered over him, six foot two inches, a good six inches taller than the waiter. Dad waited patiently, he knew the man was not happy about a youngster being there, but he just kept smiling at the back of the man's head for what seemed like an hour... Then the man looked up... Smiled as he eventually he relented.

"Okay, an extra seat for the child... " he looked round the darkened room, there were only one other couple sat at a table, "... Is this okay here?" he offered the table with an outstretched arm.

"That'll be lovely... " mum said as she took her coat off, she handed it to the waiter, who bowed slightly. She sat down and he pushed the chair in as she did, then from under his other arm he produced three menus and gave one to each of us. Then retreated, backing away slowly . Dad asked mum if she fancied a drink and then he stood again and walked to the bar, ordered himself a pint, my mum a Campari and lemonade. He turned to me and mouthed the word Coke.

"Yeah, Cokes great... But get the ice in another glass... You don't get as much Coke if they put ice in!" I shouted a little too loudly.

"Brian... Sit down and pipe down too... " she barked in a whisper... "Just get him a Coke, Bri." she said to my dad at the bar.

"I wanted ice in another glass... Then I could have added it a chunk at a time."

"You'll get what you're given... Now behave."

"Okay. Just makes sense... " I was stopped in my tracks by mum's eyes... They had begun to enlarge... It was time to step back.

Dad returned, three drinks in his enormous hands, he placed them on the table as one then divided them and placed mums and mine in front of us, he raised his glass and said, "Cheers!" then sat down heavily, took a large slug of cold lager and let out a large, "ahhhhh… " the drink had obviously been something he had been looking forward to.

"So… Anybody decided what they are having?"

"I'd like a prawn cocktail starter and the sea bass, please Bri." mum said without looking up from her menu, when she finished her order she folded the menu and smiled at dad.

"Can I have the prawn thing too, dad?" I asked sticking my bottom lip out as I finished my sentence.

"Do you even like prawns?"

"Errrr… I don't even know what a prawn is… He he" I laughed, "… Or a cocktail… Is that a chickens bum? But if mum likes it… I definitely will."

"Okay. But you had better eat it, it's not cheap… It's £1.50!!"

"I will… Thanks dad." I promised.

"Well, what are you having for your main meal?" he looked at me as he asked.

"Oh… Two meals! Flipping 'eck, brilliant. We'll have to do this more often, hey?" I studied the menu. "Er… What are mussels? Is it like these muscles?" I asked as I flexed my bicep.

"No silly, they're shellfish, Bri." mum explained.

"With what?"

"I think they come with garlic bread." mum said picking her menu up again.

"No… What are they selfish with? Do they have toys they don't share?"

"Goodness me, you really need your ear's washing out, Bri, self… Ish, not shellfish, erm… No no, shell… Fish, fish in shells." She was struggling with her own diction now.

"Okay, well I'm not having them, then, don't like the sound of that… Erm, what's Steak Diane… Or… Chicken keevs?

"Kiev. That's nice. Butter in a chicken breast." she didn't mention the butter was garlic.

"I thought he was just having burger and chips... " dad jumped in, while looking at the prices.

"Oh calm down, it's a treat. Order the food Bri." she told dad, who reluctantly lifted his arm for service.

The waiter returned, he took the orders of dad, repeating each meal back as confirmation. Dad had changed his mind and decided on the hot chicken curry much to mums dismay, I think it was the thought of garlic on me and curry and flatulence off dad that had upset her. The waiter took the menus off us, turned on a sixpence and marched off to the kitchen.

Another couple had taken seats nearby and were chatting away, mum told me to stop being nosey, and stop listening in.

"They're talking about Planet of the Apes, I want to go and see it."

"Sounds a bit daft, if you ask me." said dad.

"No... The monkeys take over the Earth and capture spacemen who've accidently landed there and they tie 'em up and the monkeys are horrible, but Charlton Heston, gets free and..."

"Oooh, Charlton Heston, I like him... It might be okay!" dad butted in.

"Can we talk about something other than monkey films please." mum had had enough.

"Football?" I suggested.

"I don't think so son... " at that moment the door opened and a small, dusty looking man walked in, mum nudged dad, "... It's Demo Don, Bri." she nodded her head in the direction of a small man, who was pulling odds and ends from his jeans pocket as he walked in, apparently looking for cash.

Dad looked over and called him across.

"Demo... Demo... " Don looked round, he looked shattered, slightly unkempt and a little lost, he smiled weakly and walked

23

across, he was about five foot six and his hair was a shorter, greyer version of Ken Dodd's.

"Hi Bri, Marie... Er... Kid." he waved at me.

"How's the wife?" dad asked.

"Still in hospital, still doesn't remember anything."

"It's so weird... Her losing her memory." mum interjected.

"Not as weird as seeing her face on the front of the Evening News... 'Woman found in Piccadilly Gardens, No memory, No Name.' Don said.

"It must have been stress." mum said in a soft voice.

"... Of living with you, Demo!" dad laughed, mum hit him.

"Brian, please. Don, you must be in a right state." she said consolingly.

"Just popped in here for a takeaway, had a few in the Museum after the hospital, but I'm alright, thanks , Marie."

"Was she abducted by aliens... Had her memory wiped, or she might have had her body swapped... Like in The Invaders, you want to check if she has a stiff little finger... The aliens can't move 'em... That's the only way you can tell they're aliens... ... What... What?" I looked round at each staring face, Don's mouth was open and I could actually see his chewing gum sat on his tongue.

"Brian, for goodness sakes, Don's wife is ill!" mum said.

"Or... Is she? If she's been abducted she... "

"Quiet... Stop being silly." I'd pushed her too far.

"Well, it's up to you... But them Invaders are nasty, they kill ya. I wouldn't be able to sleep next to her." I decided to leave it there. The three adults continued their conversation and ignored my mutterings.

I listened in on the nearby couple's conversation about Planet of the Apes while my parents consoled Demolition Don. A man appeared behind the counter and called Don. He collected his food and bade farewell to mum and dad and just sort of stared at me, once he had paid he made for the exit, waving goodbye again before disappearing.

"How dare you show me up like that?" Mum said. "Brian... Don't ignore me" she leaned across to me.

"Me? I thought you was talking to dad. What have I done?"

"Aliens!! What in God's name goes on in there?" she said pointing to my head. Dad had the biggest grin on his face. "Don't encourage him, Brian... Don will think he's not all there."

"Don's not exactly a full bob!" dad laughed.

"You see, this is how to teach a young boy how to become a delinquent."

"What's a *dequinlent*?" I asked, bemused, mum just spread her arms, as if to say, need I say more.

"He's fine, the lad's just got a vivid imagination and Don's fine too... He won't even remember what he said this time tomorrow, he's got a worse memory than his wife!" he laughed uproariously.

The door burst open and two policemen walked in, they glanced around the room and then walked purposefully across to the bar. One, the taller of the two, shouted through to the kitchen. The waiter's head popped through the door, his face changed from anger at being called to utter fear... Then a smile and then simpering.

I had turned in my chair to watch the action. The waiter had walked through the swinging door fully now and positioned himself like a barrier as the door slowly came to a stop behind him.

The taller policeman was talking down to the waiter, he pulled out a piece of paper and read something off it, the waiter shook his head, wide eyed.

The smaller policeman tried to get to the kitchen door, the waiter shifted himself to block him, putting his hands on the door jamb. The taller policeman took off his helmet, revealing his blonde hair, he put the helmet down and grabbed the waiter, picking him up and putting him to one side. The smaller cop pushed the swing door open and vanished into the steamy back room. The waiter was told to sit down and blonde cop followed his fellow officer into the kitchen.

I swung round to my parents.

"What's going on?"

"How should I know." dad answered.

"Are we safe, Bri?" mum asked my dad.

"Course we are, shhhh, let's just see what happens."

"Don't you shhhh me!!" mum said angrily.

"I'm sorry… But can we just wait and see." He said mildly.

The waiter sat on a bar stool, he was focussed on the kitchen, but occasionally he turned to smile a large, false smile into the room.

Then the kitchen door opened, two tiny Asian men in white coats exited, their arms behind their backs, both handcuffed. The policemen followed very closely behind, the blonde copper picked up his helmet as he walked. The waiter jumped from his seat.

"Hey, they're my cooks." his voice squealing.

"They were your cooks, now they're my crooks, sir." the smaller police officer joked as he pushed one of his arrestees towards the exit.

"And how am I supposed to serve the customers? Who is going to cook? You can't just take them!" his pleading fell on deaf ears as his kitchen staff, heads down, were frog marched out of the restaurant.

The waiter raced into the kitchen, then a minute later came back out. He smiled at us again then picked up the telephone off the counter. He got into a conversation that started with his explanation to someone on the other end and then an obvious explosion from the other end of the line. He pulled the red phone slightly away from his ear, and unsuccessfully trying to butt in every few seconds, but he was having no luck, the someone was not happy with him... Or the situation.

At this point dad turned away from observing a man on the point of catastrophe and made a decision.

"Time to hit the road, guys" he said, standing.

"What about the food?" mum asked, staying seated.

"Are we are not going to eat... Why have they arrested the chef's, dad?"

"I don't know why they have been arrested, but they are not coming back anytime soon." he lifted his coat from the back of his chair and began to insert an arm.

"I do not believe it... We get out once in a blue moon and we pick the night when the restaurant is raided by the Flying Squad!" mum finally accepting we were not getting fed.

The waiter tried in vain to get my dad to give him an hour to get a relief cook, even the promise of free wine could not sway him. He asked for mums coat and reluctantly he went looking for it.

Outside the evening had turned cold and the sky threatened a return to rain. We walked three abreast, dad hands in his trouser pockets, mum, arm linking him and me skipping, alongside them.

"Chippy, anyone?" dad asked.

"Oh yes, please, can I have a fish?" I twisted round and skipped backwards, looking at dad for a positive answer.

"Chippy!!" mum was not impressed, "... Chippy? It is not what I expected on our wedding anniversary, a fish and chip supper!!"

"Oooooh and can I have mushy peas too? I love mushy peas... And they're a vegetable... And I need to eat more greens... You said, mum, you know you did."

"Well, Nod, what is the options? Taxi into Manchester?" his voice betraying him, he would be more than happy with chippy.

"What is the point, nothing ever works out for me."

"Thing is, mum, me and dad will be happy, won't we dad?"
I asked naively. Dad changed his facial expression immediately.

"No, I will not, son. It was a special evening for me and your
mum and fish and chips are not special enough for your mum." I
could tell dad was hoping this would placate mum.

"You had better believe it... You will have to make this up
to me mister... I am so much better than fish, chips and mushy
peas. You can call at the outdoor and get a bottle of Mateus Rose
for me." she started to smile again.

"... And a bottle of Coke for me, dad."

"Deal... You two go on back home, I'll go and pick up the
food and drink."

"Do not pop into the vault in the Lightbowne...
Understand?" mum said this as if she was talking to a child.

"Understood... " dad agreed.

"Come on Bri, we'll go and warm the plates up, see if there
is anything good on the telly and get Trumper off the settee."

"Won't be long, Nod." dad said to mum as he strode on
down Kenyon Lane, we watched him go then took a right onto
McConnell Road.

"Why does dad call you Nod, mum?" I asked.

"Ha... The first time I ever saw your dad, it was in the
bottom Derby on Rochdale Road. I was in there with a friend
having a drink, the bar door opened and this giant of a man walked
in... The bar was packed, but every man and woman knew him.
They all waved or said hello, he was very, very charismatic."

"What does that mean, mum, that big word"?

"It means that he glowed... He stood out from every other
man in there, he always did... He always has. He was funny, tall,
good looking and I couldn't take my eyes off him... Even though
he was in work clothes, and a dirty 'donkey' jacket"

"Was that dad?"

"Yes, gosh, and it seems like yesterday!"

28

"But why Nod?"

"Ha ha, he offered to buy me a drink, I just nodded, then he started talking to me, I was very shy then, I was only twenty years old. I didn't speak a lot, hardly at all, I just nodding or shaking my head. He decided to call me Noddy from that moment... And it became Nod and it has stuck. He does make me smile, Bri, your dad... A lot." she said looking at me.

"Makes me smile tons too, mum. There's you, Nod, he calls me brush head, or bullet head. Then there's Demo Don... Everybody has a daft name... He he."

"Except your dad, he's just simply Big Bri."

"Why simply Big Bri... What does the simply mean?"

"Nooooo... It's just Big Bri... Not Simply Big Bri... Big Bri." she struggled to explain.

"And I will always be Little Bri... Won't I?" my face showed the disappointment.

"Yes, but we are all more than a name, son, you may be Little Bri, but... You can be anybody you want to be, make your own name."

"I will make my own name... Change it to Robin Daredevil I think... He he."

"Robin!!! I'm not sure I like Robin... Bit girly."

"Robin Hood!! He's not a girl"

"A man in tights... Ha ha."

"A man in... Oh yeah, I'm not going to wear tights! What about... Erm... Englebert... " I burst out laughing.

"Yeah... That will do it... Englebert Daredevil... Nobody will ever forget you... Come on Eng, let's get home get some bread buttered.

"Okay, let's hurry, it's getting cold."

A woman and her Tigger-like son, heading home on a cold, damp evening, the boy bouncing round her, yapping away, making her smile, running ahead then waiting for her to catch up... What a wonderful way to celebrate a wedding anniversary.

# JENNY GET YOUR GUN

… "Yeeharrrrr!!" it was the scream of the ten year old that made two of his older neighbours, out cleaning their front, turn and grimace. Two boys were racing down the middle of the street, it was car free and apart from the startled woman desolate.

One hand was held, extended, in front of me, it was gripping an imaginary rein, the other hand was slapping the side of my hip and the harder I hit my invisible horse, the faster it ran. Ahead, more graceful, galloping away and intermittently glancing back towards me, Stew, both shorter and lighter and with a flaming faster horse too, apparently.

"Johnny Ringo never gets beaten in a horse race, Black Bri!" he shouted at me over his shoulder.

"Black Bri?!!"… I gasped with all this exertion "Where's that come from? Am I a baddy now? I'm never the baddy! I thought we were in the same gang!"

"Yup, you are, and I am… " he started.

"… Running away from me?" I finished his sentence for him.

Stew slowed by pulling his rein arm back and up towards his chest.

"Wohhhhhh there boy… " he looked at me as I caught him up, "Get off your horse, pardner, it's time to draw!"

31

We dismounted our imaginary steeds, I wrapped my non-existent reins round the invisible wooden fencing. Then we stood back to back, I stood a good four inches taller than my older pal.

"Ten steps and turn." Stew explained.

Stewart began counting, we took the steps and by eight had looked back menacingly at each other four times, at ten we turned. I widened my stance one leg at a time, dropped both hands to my sides, the right hand slightly away from the hip, fingers clenching and unclenching, an itchy trigger finger... Stew stood 10 yards away, a mirror image... Chewing on his fictional tobacco, enhancing his character, he moved his head to the side and spat... 40% landing on his shorts!

"Oh, flippin eck... " he suddenly dropped out of that character and back into 11 year old Mancunian boy as he wiped his grey shorts rapidly with the sleeve of his olive green jumper, then he glanced from sleeve to shorts. All done.

"We drawing, or not, Jimmy Ringo?" I asked with a grimace.

"It's Johnny... It's not Jimmy... Flaming Nora, we only saw the film an hour ago, don't you remember anything, empty head?" Stew was always easily riled...

"Okay, stop whining... Johnny... Just go for your gun!"

I snapped like lightning at my hip, lifted my gun, my right hand with middle and forefinger creating the gun barrel, my thumb the hammer, at the speed of sound to a 90 degree angle and shot...

"PEEOOWWWWW" I uttered milliseconds before Stew did the same.

"Ha... You missed Hammy... But I hit you... " this must of been the reason he hadn't winced in agony... Or fell over.

I allowed him the hit... I pulled my left shoulder backwards sharply, looking round at it as I did... And stepping back at the same time, agony etched into my young face. I touched the injury gingerly then gazed at my 'bloodied' hand.

"Ha... But you only injured me!!" I might have given him a hit, but I was certainly not allowing it to be a fatal one.

I took aim again at him, my injured shoulder was drooped, but my right hand jutted out, two fingers were pointing at Stew's head, my thumb fully cocked... All ready to take him out.

"PEEEOWWWWW... Gotcha... " I walked towards him as I shot, no normal man could have survived that.

"Buuuuuttttt... You only hit my leg... " he cried out... How I hit his thigh that he gripped is beyond me... I was aiming at his flipping head. He is such a cheat... And far from the normal man!

Stew fell to the ground, rolling onto his back, his front, then his back again. On his final roll he lifted his 'handgun' and got off three quick shots at me.

My body bucked, once twice, three times... Moving left, right and then left again.

"URGGGHHHHHHHHHHHHHH!!!!!!!, you got me Jenny... Er... Johnny Ringo!!!" my hand holding my chest, face gurning in apparent painful torment, my knees began to buckle.

"Jenny!!!???" he muttered.

I swayed like a drunken sailor, I leant against the lamp post, I staggered slowly forward towards Stewart's prostrate body... And like Tchaikovsky's dying swan, I fell on top of him, knocking what small amount of air his lungs,  in that  sunken chest, could hold.

"Pfffffft... Urgh... Flippin 'eck Hammy, you nearly flamin' killed me!" he tried unsuccessfully to lift me from him.

"But you HAVE killed me Jenny Ringo!!" I laughed "I have been 'deaded' by a cowgirl, and a flipping  ugly one at that, oh, the shame, my dad will go mad at me, his son being shot by a soppy girl!"

"Heeeyy... I am not a girl, but if I was one, I bet I wouldn't be ugly, I'd  be a gorgeous one!" he decided to argue weirdly.

I then pulled my hand up holding some imaginary object... It appeared the size of an apple, I looked up at the hand, I brought the object to my mouth and I took a bite, then I spat out...

"But just before I draw my last breathe Black Bri pulls a grenade out, and the ugly Jenny can't escape... If I'm going, you are coming with me, missus"

Stew started struggling, legs kicking out. Giggling at first, then moving on to a full belly laugh as he wriggled around in my arms.

"NOOOOOOO, ha ha ha, let me go you... Haaammmmy...
"

"No escape this time Jenny, we will die together, we are off to the big prairie in the sky... BOOOOOOOOM!!!!!

# ROUGH WINDS DO SHAKE

It was an incredibly cold, but dry February afternoon, the clouds were Manchester grey, a colour just one shade away from black. The chance of sunshine before sunset was low to nil. I was on my way home from school, my hands were stuck deep into my pockets on my duffel coat, hood up to protect my ears. My thighs had taken on a purplish hue from the cold easterly wind that attacked relentlessly, its bite had icicle teeth and my socks offered little to no protection while bunched around my ankles.

I was kicking a stone about the size of a matchbox across the black, moon dust like surface of the Diggy. Twenty yards ahead was a set of goalposts, old and rickety, they leant back slightly, although they were not in danger of collapse, the concrete they had been set in had just worked a little loose, and you could pull them forward and back six inches, they wobbled like a milk tooth ready to meet the Tooth Fairy.

On the off-white posts and bar that formed the rectangular goal were bandages and several colours of sticky tape. This was the remnants of games past, used to hold keep the goal nets attached during games, as the game was finished the netting was pulled down unceremoniously then stuffed into a sack, safe until the next fixture. Some of this tape hung free and swung wildly to and fro in the icy winds.

After each kick of the stone I would follow it to where it had landed, when it had finally entered the 18 yard box and lay just to the left of the penalty spot, it was time to shoot, to score that winning goal in the F.A. Cup Final. I raced to where the stone had come to a rest, I aimed to plant my left foot just to the left of my 'ball,' and before it had hit the ground, the right foot was already being pulled back quickly and bending at the knee, and when the heel touched my buttock it swung down, hard and fast, a pendulum with a scuffed leather shoe on the end. Contact with the stone sent in flying forward towards the goal, where it hit the left upright post, causing a loud echoey metallic noise to reverberate across the dark wasteland. I threw back my head in mock shock.

Strangely, sometimes the hitting of the post brought more enjoyment than actually 'scoring' a goal. The ringing the post sang out made my heart race, and although my initial cry had to be changed mid scream, my 'Gooooawwww' still brought a smile to my face. I had even brought my hands out of my pockets to raise them to the back of my head and interlink the fingers just like the professionals did when they had missed an open goal. I was also secretly thrilled to have made my fellow homeward bound schoolchildren, suddenly slow in their stooped into the wind walk and look around. Trying to work out what had caused this clangerous noise.

I straightened up and walked through the goalposts I had been unlucky not to score in. There was a slight rise as you reached the southern end of the Diggy, then a slope down to Rudd Street. I picked up my pace a little now, it was a Wednesday so I knew Mum would be home. Charlie's, the corner shop where she worked only opened until lunch today. She would have the coal fire blazing and Trumper would be lay there warming the rug for me. I would have to move from his centre spot when i got in so I could thaw out.

Three streets fed off Rudd Street to my left, Spreadbury, Levens and then Lakin. This is where I lived, a left turn onto my street meant I was just two doors from home. I banged hard and rapidly and the door opened to reveal my mother, scowling.

"Why do you insist on banging on the door so hard? I am not deaf." I pushed through while answering her.

"You might have been on the toilet, having a wee." I explained as I squeezed by her unmoving body.

"If I was on the loo, I wouldn't have heard you outside… So it's pointless noise."

"No, but better safe than sorry, hey?" mum closed the front door behind me, confusion on her face.

"Safe from what… Hey, hey… Shoes… And coat off the floor, now!" she exclaimed.

"Awww mum, I'm frozen solid…I'll do it in a minute. Move Trumper, let me get at the fire." I turned and bent over slightly, buttocks and the back of my legs to the heat, edging my dog slightly to the left.

"Look at the colour of your legs." she said picking up my dropped items.

"I know, it's like a purply blue colour." I said looking and rubbing at my thighs.

"I meant the dirt around your ankles, have you come across the Diggy again, I've told you to walk down Brendon Avenue, it's safer and it's not dirty." she scolded me while she picked up the items I had been ordered to just moments before.

"Yeah, but it's miles further that way, and you can't expect me to freeze to death just to stay clean, can you… Here's your son, Mrs Hamblett… He's dead… But really clean… Bet you'd be happy then?" I said using Hammy logic.

"I really do not think your life would be in danger, walking three minutes longer." she said as she put my shoes in the cupboard then hung my coat on the hook on the back of the door before closing it

"But... You don't know for sure, do you? Really not worth putting my life at risk just for a speck of dirt. Is it?" I looked straight at her, showing I had faith in my statement.

"Yes I do know... Now... What have you done at school today?" changing the subject.

"Oooh... Poetry." I turned to warm my front now.

"Ahh, I love poetry, I loved learning poems when I was at school, I was the cleverest girl in my class, you know?" she beamed proudly.

"You're always saying that, bet you were dead thick really... He he." I giggled.

"Hey monkey boy!... I can still recite poems now, 25 years on."

"Go on then, do one... " I challenged her. I was bent, trying to rub heat into my reddening, chubby thighs.

"Oh, okay... Yes... Here... (small cough)... 'Shall I compare thee to a Summer's day, thou art more lovely, and more temperate. Rough winds do shake the darling buds of May, and summer's lease hath all too short a date. Sometimes too... "

"Mum... Mum... Mum... " getting louder to catch her attention, she was entranced by her own words.

"... Hot...what, what, I've not finished, Brian." she stuttered.

"But, that's not a poem, mum, it doesn't rhyme or anything."

"It's Shakespeare!"

"Well, it might be Shayspeer, but it's not a poem, is it?

"Yes, well, I think it might actually be a sonnet, but it's a form of poem, and it's lovely."

"It's just a bunch of words, and some of 'em ain't even English!" I gurned like a wide mouthed frog as I said it.

"William Shakespeare is this country's most famous writer, and he wrote some of the most famous words in history."

"Yeah, you say that, but he sounds like he made most of 'em up and to me, that's not a poet." I insisted.

"He is… " mum said defiantly.

"Well, I don't think so, poems gotta rhyme, you can't just write things down and say… Oh… I have decided this is a poem, and it doesn't rhyme, it's mad" I dug in my pocket and retrieved a piece of paper from a corner shop trip two days previous.

"Two eggs, five Park Drive,
half a pound of butter,
box of matches,
small tin of beans, and a Nimble loaf.

… There, now I've written a poem." I smiled at her.

"You, my boy, are too clever for you own good." she stared at me, trying hard to be angry, but her eyes always gave her away. "… And I wrote that list, not you… So it's my poem"

"Too clever for my own good? How can you be too clever, what's the worst that can happen by being too clever, hey? My head gets enormous 'cost me brain grown so big and explodes like a water balloon… Or… "

"Or maybe you get a thick ear for arguing with me? Tread carefully son, you are on very thin ice." her little grin saved me panicking.

"Not on ice… On a rug… He he." I only whispered this, not wanting to break the brittle ice I was metaphorically stood on.

"No one loves a smart Alec." she said.

"You said that when Uncle Ivan told you that you were wrong… Remember? When you said Ben Haggis was the highest mountain in the World."

"I didn't say Ben Haggis… I said Ben Nevis… "

"Yeah, but that's not the biggest mountain in the World either, is it?"

"What?"

"Ben Haggis isn't the biggest mountain in the World." I said this slowly as if I was talking to a person with learning difficulties.

"Apparently not… " she agreed reluctantly. "Just go and get changed now clever clogs." she'd obviously lost all patience with me.

"Okay." I walked towards the doorway to the kitchen where the stairs were, picking up a large pile of football cards off the sideboard as I walked by.

"Don't leave them on the floor upstairs, took ages getting them together this morning."

"Oh mum, are they not in order now… Flipping eck, why didn't you check the numbers first?"

"Stop it, if you leave them on the floor, think yourself lucky they are not in the bin!" she fired at me.

"Don't say that, that's an 'orrible thing to say, mum. I've been saving 'em for ages… You're just angry 'cost I said you might not be a genius"

"I never said I was a genius… And you stop being so anal about numbers…" she suddenly realised what she had said and stopped talking, she quickly turned and picked up her tea cup, she took a sip with her back to me.

"Haynul? What's haynul? Is it stupid? Are you calling me stupid?" I asked angrily, her shoulders slumped!

"Nooooo, it means… Erm, it means people who worry about things being in the right place, in order. People who stress about unimportant things like that." she smiled, happy with her explanation.

"Haynul… A person who worries too much about things being in the right place… Ha… You're haynul then!" I pointed at her as I my accusation was thrown.

"I beg your pardon!"

"You are the most haynul person I have ever met... Shoes, must go in the cupboard... Dirty plates, must go in the sink... Socks, must be balled and put in the basket... " I was walking off as I said it, leaving her opened mouthed and lost for words. "... Coats, do not leave on the floor... Underpants, not under my bed... If you lick your plate, make sure you have not left tomato sauce on your nose, chin or forehead... You see, the thing is mum, you are the haynul one, not me." I closed the door to and left her shaking her beehive hairdo in disbelief.

## KARL MALDEN'S NOSE

"Right, shush now. I want to watch this." and this was an order not a simple suggestion from my dad.

"Alright, I'm just trying to get comfortable... " I explained as I lay head in hands on the rug.

"Where's your slippers?" he asked as he watched my feet stuck up in the air, crossing and uncrossing.

"Er... " I scanned the living room slowly. Trumper wandered in on cue from the kitchen, one slipper in his mouth. "... Trump's eating one... So I'm not putting that on my foot with all his slavva on it."

"Put it down by the fire to dry... Then find your other one... And quickly!"

"Here Trumps... " I put my hand out to retrieve it.

"Shush!!"

"Flipping 'eck... Just asking him to bring me my slipper... It's not even started properly"

"Would you like me to get my slipper and slap your backside with it?" he failed to get the venom he wanted into the threat.

"Ha ha... Smack me... Just for talking. You can't beat a child just for chatting with his dog... That's just mad, and probably illegal!!"

"If you're talking at the start of Streets of San Francisco... I will beat you, legal or not." he insisted feebly.

42

I got up, dragged the soft, brown checked slipper from my dog's mouth and laid it down in front of the coal fire. Then walked to the kitchen to retrieve the other.

"Bri... Bring me the bottle opener, please." he called.

I rattled through the cutlery drawer until I spotted the tin opener with added bottle top flipper on the handle.

"... And close the drawer after you." he added.

"I already have... " I lied, then tried ever so carefully to close it without him hearing me.

"Course you have... Ha ha... " he said sarcastically.

"I had closed it... So I don't even know what you're laughing at." I said as I reappeared in the doorway. The iconic music had begun and Karl Malden's face was on the screen followed closely by Michael Douglas.

"Here... " he took the bottle top opener from me, "... Sit down now...and shut up!" he popped the top off a bottle of Newcastle Brown ale and began to pour, the froth bubbled up and threatened to flow over the lip of the glass. Quickly he put his finger on the rim and bubbles stopped suddenly, not a drop was lost.

"How does that work dad?" I asked.

"What?" he glared at me then straight back to the television.

"Your finger stopping the froth... "

"Oils on the skin... They pop the bubbles... Like what Fairy Liquid does."

"I haven't got oily skin... And I didn't know you had."

"You need oil in your skin so you don't turn to dust... ", exasperation increasing.

"So if..."

"So if... You shut up... I can watch this!." he said pointing the bottle opener at the screen.

"How am I ever supposed to learn if I can't ask a question... ?" I muttered under my breath.

"How am I supposed to know what's going on in San Francisco if you don't put a sock in it?"

"Shame I haven't got a boomerang that can stop time!" I said, a heavy breath exhaled slowly at the end of my sentence.

"What are you on about now?"

"The Magic Boomerang... When I was small there was a program on telly about a boy who threw a boomerang and stopped time... Everyone froze, apart from him, while it was in the air." I explained.

"Sounds thrilling... But you haven't got one. So unless you want to go to bed... Zip it."

"Okay... " the silence lasted fifteen seconds, "... Why is he doing that?"

"I don't know... I haven't seen it before, have I?"

"Just seems a bit daft, he's going to hurt someone if he's not careful... "

"I'm going to bloody hurt someone if they're not careful and shut up."

"Sorry... " I rolled my eyes, "bet he hurts someone though." I whispered. "You watch!"

A semi silence broke out until end of part one, when I asked if I could get my walnut whip, and dad asked me to fetch his other Newcastle Brown from the fridge.

I sat on the floor with my back against the arm of his chair, an orangey coloured chair that had the feel of suede. I opened up the wrapper and removed my walnut whip, I looked at it with both love and disgust.

"What is the point of having a brilliant sweet like this... " I lifted it into my dad's eyeline, "... Then sticking a flipping walnut on it?"

"Here... I'll have it." dad grabbed it from my fingers and popped the walnut into his mouth, then handed me my conical chocolate back.

"Urghhh… They're horrible… They're not real food." I said in disgust.

"Good for your brain. Now, they have got oil in them." he said.

"Yeah… But wouldn't it make more sense if you stuck a fruit pastille on the top… That would be brill." my eyes lit up at the idea of the perfect confectionary.

"Shush now… It's back on… "

"How can he be an actor with a nose like that?" I asked this then took an enormous bite causing the chocolate to crack and break and vanilla fondant to pop into view.

"What has a nose got to do with being an actor?" dad asked.

"Well… I can't concentrate on what he is saying… I just keep thinking someone has exploded some bangers up his nostrils!" I looked up and back at my dad, he was smiling and bringing his beer to his mouth. "It is the horribliest nose I have ever seen… Bet you have never seen a nose like that… Have you?"

"Well, no, but he is still a good actor… And you are a complete barmpot!" he put his glass to his mouth and drained half of it in two gulps.

"Oh no I'm not… And you know I'm telling the truth… His nose has even got a centre parting… He he."

"Shush… " he began the task of catching up with the plot again.

"Mum says your nose'll go like that if you carry on drinking so much!"

"What. Two glasses of beer? Wait until she gets back from bingo!. I'll have you know I have a very distinguished nose, and it's staying that way." he stroked his forefinger down the front of it, while lifting his chin, like a Roman Emperor or English Mussolini.

"Distinkwished would that mean massive?… Ha ha?"

"Hey you cheeky swine... It's not that big." San Francisco was on the back burner for now.

"Not on your head it's not... But if it was on a normal sized head it would look like an eagle's beak... He he."

"You have got the same nose, bullet head, so I would shut up now, before you get yourself in trouble..." he then looked back at the telly, "... Now... What's he been arrested for? I've lost track here, watching telly with you is a nightmare!"

"Is he the one who was driving the bus?" I placed my sticky finger on a man's face on the screen.

"What bus?" he stared down at me. "Get your fingers off... Look at that now... Fingerprints on the telly!"

"Oh no, sorry, that was on Please Sir before... But he does look like him, doesn't he?" I said, wiping the television with my pyjama sleeve.

"How would I know? I can't see through you! Can you shut up and move or go to bed... I can't rewind the telly and watch it again." exasperation dripping from every word.

"Be great if you could... Can you imagine a machine that let you... What... What?" I was stopped mid-sentence by the burning of his eyes into my head.

"QUIET!!!"

"Okay. But can you scratch my head?" I crawled back to his chair and put my head by his knee.

He lay his heavy hand on my thick, black mop of hair and his four fingers began a gentle scratch cum massage, it relaxed me and to a certain extent him. I carried on eating my walnut whip, little bits of chocolate falling onto my pyjamas and pondered writing to the makers of my confectionary with my idea of ditching the walnut, then decided I would wait until I grew up and make my own more pastilley version and steal their market, I'd become a millionaire with the fruit pastille whip. Then I would invent a box that would make television program go backwards so you never had to miss anything on telly again.

Even if she had a son who drove her up the wall, she could be proud I was super rich... And she never had to miss an episode of Coronation Street again!

## THE BIG CHEESE

"Ha... Let's have a look... " I leaned across the dining table in Kath's living room, my hand held out to collect the item for my scrutiny.

"Careful, don't drop it, it's the only one I've got." Geoff Marsden handed me the coin.

"Sooo... This is not a bob anymore... It's a five new pence?" I looked up from the coin to see him nodding in confirmation.

"... And all the old bobs, tanners, half-crowns... All of 'em are going?"

"Yep, it's a whole new world, Hammy... All the old people will be having a fit in the Co-op... Ha ha."

"Why?"

"Old people don't like anything new... Colour telly... Rubbish... Georgie Best... You should of seen Duncan Edwards... Raquel Welch... Not as pretty as Rita Hayworth... Cars... Not as good as donkeys... Ha ha... They think anything new is crap...they can't help it." he put his hands behind his head, big smile on his face, confident in his information.

"Will we think new things are cr... Er... Rubbish when we get dead old too?" I wondered out loud.

"Yep... We will hate jet packs... Giant televisions... Robots... Flying cars... We will hate 'me all." he was rocking on the back legs of his chair now, looking like the oracle.

"I won't... " I piped in quickly, "Giant telly's and robots, it'll be brilliant... I want a robot that can sing... Do you think they'll make one?"

Kath's head suddenly appeared at the kitchen door.

"Are you watching this stupid cricket... Or not?" she asked.

"Course we are. It's the Gillette Cup Final, mum... Tsk." Geoff answered as if it was probably the daftest question of the day... Even though I'd been bothering him all morning.

"Fine, but I'm turning it off if you're not... How's your soup, Brian, nice?"

"It's lovely Kath... What is it again?" I put another spoonful into my mouth and made a yummy face.

"Oxtail... " she smiled and immediately disappeared back into the kitchen.

"Oxtail... Like from next to the cows bum?" Geoff whispered to me, then smiled, daring me to swallow.

Heavy, plodding footsteps on the stairs made me turn to see who was about to enter... Debbie, Paula, Karen, Ant or little Dave. The door opened and it wasn't any of them, it was Bill and he was the dad and he always made me smile on a Saturday morning, a vest on... His shirt tucked into his trousers but hanging down like a white skirt over his backside. He ruffled my hair as he passed and asked if I was okay... Insisting on referring to me as 'ugly.'

"I'm okay, Bill, are you?"

"I will be as soon as I've had a shave and escaped this madhouse!" I looked around, all was calm... All was quiet, I'd seen madder! He walked into the kitchen and returned moments later with a mug, a small brush, a stick of shaving soap and a safety razor.

I had watched my dad shave several times and I was becoming aware that each man had his own shaving routine and style, dad using foam from a can... Bill took time to build suds on his brush in a circular motion on the soap... Dad always started near his left ear... Bill from the Adam's apple up... And he also pinched his nostrils when shaving round his nose, looking like he was trying to lift himself off the floor. Dad always shaved in the bathroom while whistling a lively tune and always within minutes of waking... Loo first then bathroom, every morning, come rain or shine.

Bill on a Saturday morning would stand in front of the living room mirror, water mug on the mantelpiece and he would scrape the hair off his face, I would always smile in the winter when the roaring coal fire would be too fierce for his legs and he would have to retreat to the kitchen or the bathroom.

Some Saturday morning I would go to the Marsden's to play, watch television and be fed, this happened when mum was working at Charlie's, the corner shop, and dad was still lost somewhere on the U.K. road network, delivering anything from dolls to sheet metal, sometimes in a flatbed truck but, more often than not, in his forty foot container, articulated, heavy goods vehicle.

"Brian... Do you want to play house?" my head snapped to my left, Paula was stood at my shoulder with two dolls and a small blanket... And to her, playing was pretending to be my wife!!

"Er... I don't think so Paula, you do know I'm a boy, don't you, we really don't like that sort of thing?" I turned back to Geoff and tutted... "girls!!" Geoff smiled and tried to push me off my chair. "... Hey!"

"But it'll be fun... " Paula replied, "... You can be my husband... And these two can be our babies. Sarah and Derek!"

Paula was just a few months younger than me and like a sister, she offered up the two dolls for my perusal... One with an eyelid that was permanently shut, the other that had a felt tip moustache painted across its top lip and both suffering with the worst case of alopecia I would ever encounter... And she wanted these to be my children! If I ever had kids they were going to have a full head of luscious dark hair, both will be gorgeous and neither of them called Derek... Just like me.

"... Paula... I have no intention of being married to you or anyone, pretend or not. Now, if you want a game of 'split the kipper or 'slapsy's' I'm your man... But you'll have to ask your mum to lend us a big, sharp knife.".

"I'm not playing with knives... It's dangerous... We can get a blanket and put it down on the grass outside... Have a tea party... Take the babies for a walk in the pram" she suggested with a girly smile.

"Sorry, it's still a no... What about you Geoff... Split the kipper?" Paula's face dropped as I turned away.

"How's about you give me my new money back before we go any further?" Geoff insisted.

"Oh aye... He he... I've somehow put it in my pocket, it'll be because your Poo has been mithering me with her Hammer House of Horror dolls... But it was an accident though, Geoff, honest injun... You know I'm not a thief... " an innocent smile came to my lips.

"You would have been a dead thief if you'd tried to leave this house with it in your pocket... " he promised with his spoon held up, dagger style. The fact it wasn't the sharpest piece of cutlery and it was sending thick Oxtail soup slowly down his arm and into his sleeve, took the edge of this intended threat.

"Brian, is your dad going in the Lightbowne?" Bill thankfully interrupted, I turned, leaving Geoff to finally realise he had a river of soup heading to his elbow.

"Mum said he only got back from Glasgow at 3 this morning, Bill... So I think he'll be in bed for a bit yet."

"He's a right big girls blouse... Saturdays are for beer and cards... You can lie in bed after your tea" he laughed, he was now pulling his shirt up and feeding his arms into the sleeves, he lifted his braces over his shoulders and started on the buttons.

51

"Me dad said you're rubbish at cards... And he likes taking your wages off you... He he." I giggled.

Kath stepped out of the kitchen again, dirty laundry held under her left arm.

"Everybody takes his bloody wages off him... Apart from me! Boy's, bring your plates into the kitchen when you're done... I hope you haven't left any." her right index finger pointing at each of our plates alternately.

I looked down at my brown, meaty soup and dipped in another piece of thick, well-buttered bread, brought it up to my mouth quickly, bending forward so as not to let drips get on the plastic table cloth.

"What is it?" Bill asked, his face grimacing at the look of the soup.

"Ox's tail... " I said, my chin and nose wet with soup from the bread.

"You know why it's brown, don't you?" he asked me.

"Cos the meat's brown?"

"No... Because the ox wipes his bum with its tail... " his eyebrows jumped and his eye's widened. I felt a little reflux... Why do dads insist on making you feel as uncomfortable as they do?

"Thanks, but Geoff's already told me I'm eating poo soup!!" I shook my head and decided enough was enough... Geoff and dad shared a smile.

There was only a couple of spoonful's left in the bowl when I got into the kitchen. Kath had a twin tub washing machine shaking away, a grey pipe was purging dirty water from the machine into the sink. The noise of the spin cycle was intense and when it reached maximum revolutions it actually began to move across the kitchen, rocking and sidling along.

Kath was bent low, taking the machine in a two handed grip in an attempt to restrain its movement... She looked like a tall slender wrestler trying to pin down a small, squat Les Kellet in a war of attrition... This image would make me smile later when I watched World of Sport later that evening.

I placed the white soup bowl on the light blue Formica kitchen table, because the sink was not available to any pots at that moment, Kath was busy on her clothes washing, and pots would come later for her.

When I think about her now, it's hard to remember her ever sitting down and relaxing... She was always on the go.

"That was lovely Kath... " I lied... Geoff's comments had not helped.

"Sorry, one minute, Brian." she raced out of the kitchen shouting after her husband, she'd thought he was leaving but there he was, still preening himself by the living room mirror, combing his thinning, brylcreemed locks into position.

Alone, sat on the table was the biggest piece of cheese I have ever seen... Six inches high... And I loved cheese. I saw a small chunk had broken off and looking round and seeing no-one watching I popped it into my mouth. Kath walked back in milliseconds later. Eeek! I clamped my lips shut.

I looked into her eyes, with my newly acquired hamster cheeks.

"Was the soup nice?" she asked, lifting a bundle of wet clothes out of the twin tub. I nodded, trying to see an escape route past her.

"Now look at this, didn't I say don't leave any?" she nodded at the remnants of soup in the bowl. She wasn't angry, more disappointed. She placed the wet clothes in an empty plastic basket. The pipes that ran from the machine blocked that exit... Kath and her washing obstructed me the other way.

I nodded... And held my stomach with both hands, indicating fullness. At this point I started to realise the cheese was not the normal Cheddar or Cheshire variety... Although of the same texture... The taste was of something quite obscene.

I wanted to escape but she was blocking my exit... This cheese was disgusting... I mean really, really disgusting. She turned the tap over the sink counter clockwise and you could hear the water coursing down the attached plastic pipe, filling the left sided tub with the clothes in. She pointed at the cheese on the plate. My eyes widened... Had she realised I stolen some?

"Pass me that block of soap, Brian, please!" SOAP!!!! Wide eyed, I lifted the plate. I slowly passed the plate to Kath, the soap in my mouth was now starting to react with my saliva... And I was unable to swallow.

I watched as she lay a number of dirty shirts over the back of chair, then one by one began forcing the soap across the inside collar, she said she wouldn't be a minute and I'd be able to get back to the living room... I debated spitting out the soap, but decided to suffer because of the embarrassment... It really had been too long now. I just suffered as the horrific taste of washing soap discovered each and every individual taste bud in my mouth, and coated them in their entirety. It was something that was going to taint the flavour of my next five hundred meals.

"You want to get through now?" she asked, smiling as the last shirt collar was pre-soaped before going into the washing machine ... Did she know?... Had she blocked my exit just to teach me a lesson? If she hadn't done it on purpose... Then God certainly had.

I nodded wildly and squeezed past her... Gagging, I bolted through the living room, nodding pleasantly at the dolls that Paula held up before me, smiling maniacally at Bill as he gazed at me through the reflection of the mirror, completely ignored Geoff when he asked me if I fancied a game of blow football... And leapt up the stairs... Two at a time, pulling on the bannister with my left hand, whilst at the same time emptying the foaming and moist hunk of yellow soap into my right.

I opened the bathroom door and burst in, locked it behind me, my tongue was already out and begging for mercy... The cold tap was turned on full and I draped it under... Pulling it as far out as possible with the forefinger and thumb of one hand while scraping, with the nails of the four fingers of the other, from the back to the tip... I pulled a tube of toothpaste down into the sink and squeezed a dollop on my finger, spreading it all across the surface... There was a temporary relief... Then seconds later into just became a minty soap taste! I looked round in silent hysterics and tried to find something that would clean it thoroughly... ... Hah hah... A nail brush...or a loofer!... I grabbed at the nail brush first... The loofer would be a last ditch implement.

Mum would have been proud of me... It was the first time I had taken it upon myself to actually use a nail brush independently... True, it was probably the first time anyone had used one on their tongue... But as they say... Baby steps... Tongue today... Nails... Next year... Maybe!

I gagged about ninety four times... Dry heaving, moving to the lavatory several times in case of projectile vomiting... But eventually... Some ten minutes later my tongue was unable to detect the taste of carbolic... In fact it was several weeks until I recognise the taste of anything! I suspect I had managed to defoliate each and every taste bud... My own personal 'Agent Orange.'

I wandered downstairs, behind Debbie in her nightie, still half asleep and completely oblivious to me... And my watering eyes.

When I re-entered the living room, Geoff inquired if I had honked up or had the runs. I explained I'd had an upset stomach, which instantly worried him as we had eaten the same lunch. He told his mother who came in, double quick, with a bottle of castor oil... I backed away slowly, hands up trying to cover my mouth.

Minutes later I had taken a spoonful and my fears had been groundless... No taste buds... No horrible after taste. Indeed I had eventually impressed the whole family with my willingness to have a second spoonful... When I say impressed... Kath thought I was just being greedy... The rest just suspected I was not, as per usual, playing with a full deck of cards.

By the end of the day Lancashire had beaten Sussex, I'd manage to stab poor Paula in the foot playing split the kipper, I had been annihilated 10-3 by Geoff in blow football and had my bowels completely cleaned out by the castor oil... I'd sat on our outside loo reading the Dandy, Beezer and Topper for two hours solid (only thing solid happening in there!) having a 1971 version of a colonic irrigation!

Halcyon days, indeed!

## Two Little Words

"Are you okay son, you didn't eat all your tea and you didn't want any supper, you feeling alright?"

"Yeah, well, no...yeah." my answer had confused my mum slightly.

She had just tucked me in bed and said goodnight, but my insipid, muddled reply had left her wondering about my frame of mind.

"Well, are you poorly or is there a problem at school that's worrying you?" she sat down on the edge of my bed as she spoke then leant in to me, her big caring eye's carrying a touch of worry.

"Not really poorly, but, oh it's nothing really, it's just something someone said."

"Something nasty?" her face scrunched up slightly as she scrutinised my features in the gloom.

"Not nasty, just teasing really, and I shouldn't get upset at a little teasing, should I? I said in a soft voice.

"What have they said?" she asked.

"Nothing, it doesn't matter. It's all over now. Sticks and stones and all that... " I rolled over to face the wall.

"Tell me, come on, no need for you to have this on your mind before sleep son. Tell me and you'll feel a lot better, a problem shared is a problem halved" she promised.

"Oh, don't bring maths into it, I'm rubbish at maths! Just leave it, it's silly" I was still speaking to my wallpaper of war planes.

"It's not maths, Brian and it's not silly if it's still in your head at bedtime."

"Other kids get teased, and it's just my turn, I expect... 'spose every kid'll get teased 'bout something, won't they?"

"Big bullies rarely get teased, son... They are the ones who do the teasing... Nasty little thugs." she put her arm on my shoulder and pulled me onto my back again.

"It's a girl!" I mumbled.

"Pardon son, it's who?" she hadn't heard the words in my whisper, she leaned in closer.

"It's a girl... " a little louder, enough to make my mother's eyebrows raise in surprise and for her to sit back up.

"A girl! Oh dear, what has she said, Bri?" trying to hide her surprise, but failing miserably.

"Er... The school class party... We had to choose partners for a dance and no one would be my partner, and a girl said I was too fat." my eye's filled a little, not full on crying, the sort of tears that make your eye's glisten like precious stones, there's always something irresistible  about them, especially to a mother.

"Fat, give over... You are joking, son. You are not fat, you're very tall, and you look lovely." she answered then kissed my cheek.

"You have to say that though. You're my mum, you have to love me."

"I do... That's true... But, and Bri, and this is a big, big but..."

"Is it as big as my big butt?" I smiled weakly.

"Stop that, and stop it now... You are loved, not just by me and your Dad, but there's Nana, Granddad, all your Aunties, Sue, Jen, Marg, and all the rest, your Uncles, everybody I know thinks you are the perfect son... Apart from... When you and Stewart are up to your games... But even then you don't really intend to burn things to the ground or upset people with your catapults, you're both just a little clumsy, but 'you' love people... And they love you back." she was desperately trying to rest my mind.

"But... It's just a little but this time, these are all people who have to like me... They are my relations... And it's easier to love your family... Even some of Stews family think he's alright sometimes. I suppose this is the silly thing, I have lots and lots of nice things said by so, so, so many, really nice people, and kind people who I would like to grow up to be like and it is brill hearing the nice things and getting all them big hugs. So why is it that when someone that is a little bit cruel, that you don't even like, that always annoys the teacher, that aren't that clever in class, that walk in the middle of your footy game just to get on everybody's nerves, why is it when they say just two little words like... 'he's fat,' why does that stay in your head, why does that manage to beat all the loves, loads of hugs or a smashing kiss off your mum, why is it horrible stronger than nice?" I looked up after my ramble, my eyes were now dry but imploring an answer.

"Phew... Look, the girl probably doesn't know how much she has hurt you. The two words are little, but they are words that have talons," I looked at her for an explanation, "... Talons... Er... Like a tiger's nails, sharp and when they stick in you... Well they are hard to get out of your skin. Yeah?" I nodded. "Now... Those words can only work if you let them, if you called Stewart stupid, would he be upset?"

"No... He doesn't think he is... Which shows how daft he really is... He he." I replied.

"So there it is... The problem is only a problem because you are letting it be a problem. Do you... " she pointed slowly at my prostrate body, "... Do you think you're fat?" she looked softly down at me.

"Erm... Yeah... I am a little... I've got a bit of a belly... And I've got... " mum intervened.

"Enough, you are wrong, so very, very wrong. People come in all shapes and sizes, and at your age you have not yet developed. Life has yet to reveal your true body... And well... Is your dad fat? Am I fat? No... Don't answer that... " she joked.

"You will be a tall, very handsome boy then a gorgeous man eventually, and that silly girl will look at you when she grows up and not understand why you don't want to kiss her." I made a face like I was sucking lemons. "I want you to understand son, I am not and never will put you on any silly diet, but if that girl is more important than a glass of Tizer you can have water with your meals... If her stupid words are more relevant than cheese and onion crisps, then we can cut back on them too... Not a diet... Just less treats... Okay?"

"Okay, will I be thin then... And what's 'revelant' mean?" I had sat up now, my weight on both elbows.

"The word is relevant, son... And it just means important, do her words mean more than the crisps... And no, you are not going to be slimmer straight away... You really don't want to be thin... Boney... Urghhhh... Nothing worse than a skinny man, look at your dad, big, strong, handsome... And definitely not thin!" as she spoke the smile on her face grew, her focus became a little distant as she described the man of her dreams... My dad.

"I 'spose... " It was impossible to disagree.

"No supposing about it, Bri... Is your dad thin? And does anybody not like your dad? You will grow up like him, and you will be as happy as he is."

"No, everyone loves him... Even if he is a bit daft. I think I'd be happy to grow up like my dad... "

"There now, do you feel a little better?"

"Think I'll feel really better when I lose a bit of weight... But I'm not as sad as I was." I struggled to pull my arms out of the tightly tucked in cotton sheets and held them up towards her for a hug.

My dad voice suddenly called came from the bottom of the stairs.

"There's a cup of tea here, Nod, and it's going cold." my dad's voice was soft but carried easily up to my room.

"Okay, I'll be down in a minute, I'm just finishing off saying goodnight to Bri." she then turned and smiled at me. "Now, before I go, 1… Only listen to people you respect. 2… Disregard the nasty words anyone says about you… And just as importantly, about anyone else. Even though the words are not capable of leaving a scar, you now know that horrible words can bruise your heart… And lovely words can just as easily warm it. Finally, 3… Let's cut back on crisps, Tizer and butties."

"Woahhhh… Hang on a minute. I never agreed to not having butties, we can start with crisps and Tizer… See how that goes… But I really don't want to end up falling down a grid, do I? He he."

"Good lad, and good night. Any problems in future, you tell me, we then sort the problem out quickly, and it doesn't leave a cloud over you… Right, time to go to sleep… " another kiss, to the forehead this time. She rose and walked to the door, a final turn and her lovely smile shone through the gloom.

"I know I'm 'only' family!" she laughed gently. "… But I love you more than anything on this planet, son, even that big man downstairs, only just, mind… And I know you said I have to say it, but… And this is the very biggest but of the evening… I really love loving you." she just stood there for a second, then came a little wave and she'd gone.

"Leave the landing light on, please… … " I called as she left my door slightly ajar. "I love being loved by you!" I whispered to where she had stood seconds before, then turned to Trumper, who had lay, motionless across my feet throughout the Mum and son conference... "Hey, I love you too, you big fat, hairy, smelly, lovely dog... He he... You don't mind, do you, you know I don't mean it."

"Woof... " this was more like he was just clearing his throat, than a bark of understanding, he had barely had the energy to lift his head and his eyes were half closed, he then dropped it into his paws again, exhausted and like me, ready to slip this mortal coil for the night.

## OUT OF THE MOUTHS OF BABES

"Hey... Why's it so dark in here? Why are the curtains closed, mum?" I asked as I walked into the living room, a thickly buttered piece of toast halfway to my mouth.

"Mrs Smith has died!" mum explained in a whisper, as if she didn't want anyone else to know.

"Ahhh... Do the curtains stop her ghost getting in then?" a reasonable question I thought.

"No silly, it's just showing respect"

"Respect... What, by hiding?" A quizzical look spread slowly across my face.

"We're not hiding, Brian, it's just what you do when a neighbour or friend passes on." she was still using a very soft tone of voice.

"Where she passed on to?"

"Oh Brian, she has gone to heaven."

"When does she actually get into heaven, is it as soon as she closes her eyes?" I finally managed a bite of my toast, tearing it as soon as I clamped my teeth on the bread.

"Errr... Yes, don't talk with your mouth full, please?"

"Sorry," food still being chewed as I chomped."... Does Jesus meet you... Or is it God?"

"NO... It's your friends and loved ones, son, they are there to make you feel safe and cared for."

"So what if none of your friends are dead... Or your mum or dad?" a worried look spread across my brow.

"Well you have Grandparents in heaven... There is always someone... " she tried to calm my worries.

"Well... " eyes closed, bottom lip sticking up towards my nose in thought, "... I hope I don't die yet mum... Every one of my friends are here, and everyone I love is still alive... You, dad, the Marsy's, Stew all my Aunties... Sue, Jen, Marg, Jean and Mary. Then there's Gud... And all my Uncles... Me Nana, Granddad... Georgie Best... Oh... And Trumper as well!"

"Oh Brian." Mum leant down and pulled me in to the squeeziest hug.

"Mum... Mum... I... Can't... Breathe... " I gasped

"Sometimes Brian you just make me love you more... "

"More than what... ?"

"Just more than before... " she explained.

"Mum, if all my friends and all my loved ones that are supposed to meet me when I get to heaven are still alive, like all of mine are ... Does that mean that this could be my heaven... In Moston?!!!!!!"

"Mum, muuum, muuuuuuum... Your squeezing even harder... Flippin eck, you're breaking me back, mum, I can't breathe... Mum?... Are you crying mum?... Have I been norty or summfin mum?... Mum... You lost your voice?... Mum?

## DANCE LIKE NO ONE IS WATCHING

"We need to do something different, something we haven't played for ages... And ages?" I was lay on a garage roof on the Diggy. My hands were behind my head and I was enjoying the early Sunday morning sun. I was speaking to my 'frenemy' (half friend/half enemy) Stew, who was peeing, using his right hand to guide a long stream of urine over the edge of the roof and down into a half empty paint tin that sat on the ground between us and the next garage.

He looked over his shoulder at me... "Er... We played Robin Hood a few days ago... Remember? We also made little Dave Marsy wear a dress and pretend he was Joan of Arc, yesterday... Then you wouldn't let me burn him at the stake!"...

"Oh yeah, I wonder why not??"

"I wouldn't have really burnt him to death, I would have just started a little fire and got a picture of him screaming!""

"Yeah... Yeah... If Bill and Kath found out you would have been for the high jump!"

"Yip, anyway, had no matches!" he had finished his golden shower and tucked himself away. He zipped himself up, wiped his damp right hand on his grey shorts and leapt across the small gap to the white corrugated roof of the next garage.

"Good job... Bill would have killed you... Proper killed too."

"Told you, I wouldn't really of set him on fire… " he walked up to the apex of the roof, leaning slightly forward, he balanced on the ridge, arms outstretched, swaying slowly one way then the next like a tightrope walker.

"… What about Beverly Hillbillies? I laughed… "Texas Tea!"

"You mean try digging for oil?" he turned quickly as he asked, stumbling as he lost his footing on a groove.

"No… I was only joking… Where the 'eck would we dig?" I laughed out loud, but at the same time imagining me and Stew stood, spades in hand, looking at each other with the World's biggest grins on our young faces as crude oil bubbled over our toes from our very first plunge into Mother Earth.

"What about detectives? I've actually just read Emil and the Detectives… "

"You? You read a book… Did you read it all!" he looked shocked.

"Yeah… An all the way through, too!" lifted my head to see how impressed he was.

"I'm only going to read books on vampires… Or the rise of the Third Reich" Stew said as he slowly brought his left leg out and round and placed it down again in front of him, his swaying was erratic now as he tight-roped walked along… Jerking his little body one way then the next, fighting to stay upright. Then suddenly he found his centre and steadied himself, arm movement now minimal, but still outstretched in his crucifix stance. He turned his head in my direction, so I was now in his peripheral visual field.

"I can't play anything, now… I've got to go somewhere with me mum?"

"Where?"

"Nowhere important… Just gotta go."

"Is it the same place as last week?" I enquired.

"You've got a really big nose, haven't you." Stew said, obviously not wanting to tell me where he was going.

"You've got boney knees!" I spat back.

"I meant... Keep your nose out... Or it might get bit off!" he threatened.

"You going to Belle Vue Zoo... ?

"What are you on about?"

"You said I might get my nose bit off... So, you might be wrestling crocodiles... Or sticking your head in a lion's mouth... Flipping 'eck... Can I watch?"

"No, I am not going to the zoo, and I'll be the one biting your nose off... So mind your own business... Putting my head in a lions mouth... I'll put your head in the bog. I've gotta go" with that Stew bent to his left and ran away from me, down the far side of the white roof and leapt across to the next garage, slowed, then climbed that, repeating the act of up, down... Leap... Over 4 more garage roof., He reminded me of Spiderman, without the web... Or the suit... Or any Spidey Sense! Then he reached last one, like a cat, agile and lithe and with all nine lives still intact... He literally took a leap of faith, jumping into fresh air with a loud whoop, then landing his knees collapsing instantly, then he performed a forward roll... Perfect Paratrooper style and he rose and dusted himself down... Olga Korbut would have been impressed.

I, on the other hand, gingerly reached the edge of my roof, sat down and dangled my legs over the edge. Twisting my body, I rolled over onto my stomach and inch by inch I began my journey towards Terra Firma.

If Stew was the cat, I was the sloth, I now hung down off the roof, my jumper snagged on something. It had ridden up to my chin and I worried I was going to be strangled by it. My legs kicked and searched for purchase, trying to get back up, my arms were not strong enough to pull me up and without a ledge to take my weight I was scared where this would end.

67

"Stew… STEWWWW!!" I called.

"Just drop." he said, I couldn't see him, I couldn't see anything, and the jumper was over my face now.

"It might hang me… "

"Nah, it'll just come off… " he insisted.

I hung there for ten seconds, playing through my head what was below, a brick?. I could twist my ankle on that. That paint tin?. I could tread on that and be covered in Stew's pee, and how far was the actual drop? I looked down… It was only 18 inches! Time to let go.

I dropped like a bag of wet sand, my jumper staying attached to the garage and peeled from my torso, both arms slipping free. This was the polar opposite of Stews descent, no grace… No dexterity… No decorum. I sat, topless on a green, plastic watering can, I'd split it and now had the look of a street vagabond with incontinence… My jumper waving in a breeze above my head.

"You've wet yourself… Ha ha.?" Stew laughed, I looked up to see him bent double.

"It's not funny… I'm soaked… You didn't pee in this, did you?

"No… Ho… Wish I had now, though" his laughter getting even more raucous.

* * *

By the time we had reached the back gate to my house, I had gained no more information from him, he was adamant it had nothing to do with me… And I was to stay in the dark.

"Right, might see you tonight, taraa" Stew said, he stuck his hands in his pocket and made his way home, he didn't look happy at all.

It didn't take me long to decide that I needed to find out what Stewart was up to on our Sunday afternoons, I hate being out of the loop on anything, even now, forty years later.

The plan was basic... I would follow him... Nice and simple... A little bit of detective work. So forty five minutes later, having had my head stuck to my parents' bedroom window finally paid dividends. Out of Stews door, half way up the street on the opposite side, Stew walked out, followed by his mother. She pulled the door shut, gave it a shove to make certain she had locked it securely then they both walked out of my sight up Lakin Street. I flew down the stairs, put on my shoes the best I could... The back of the right shoe was collapsed under my heel.

"Put your shoe on properly, Brian!" mum scolded me.

"I will, I will... In a minute... I've gotta go."

"Take Trumper... He needs some fresh air and a walk."

"Awww mum, I'm doing some detectiving stuff."

Mum looked at me and put her hands on her hips, a tea towel hanging from her left fist.

"Whose dog is he?" Trumper looked from mum to me... Then back to mum.

"Mine... Where's his lead?" I said defeat dripping from every word.

"Here... Make sure he does his stuff somewhere no one will walk in it... " she said with a little embarrassment.

"Okay... Poo on the Diggy... Gotta go now... Bye... Come on dog." all this was said as I hobbled, banging my foot in an attempt to get the shoe to go on properly.

"Brian, just put the shoe on properly, please, stop the messing about."

"Alright... But I'm in a rush... Trumper come on... " Trumper could not have been more reluctant... You'd have thought he was going to the vets to be 'fixed!'

We raced up the street, at the top I dipped my head round the corner... Stew and mother were making their way up past the scout hut... Calculations began in my head... Lightbowne Road and Kenyon Lane... Or Diggy and McConnell Road the other possible route. Pincer movements are not so easy when there is only one of you.

Kenyon Lane won... So we raced down Douglas Street, across the tree laden area to the rear of the Church Chapel... Trumper produced a dog egg... Then onward. A left onto Kenyon Lane. I set up a steady jog... Past the Conservative Club on the right, the Adelphi bingo hall on our left... This was a large and imposing building, off white and all Art Deco. I slowed to a brisk walk now... Two hundred yards ahead were two figures, mother and child. The child's head hung low and his hands stuck firmly in his trouser pockets. His body language gave away his demeanour... Wherever he was going... He didn't want to go.

"Stay Trumper! Now you can be Watson... And I'll be Hamlock Holmes... the World famous child detective... He he." I knelt by his side and watched them cross the road and head to St Dunstan's hall... Through the gate and up the steps into the hall itself.

"What are they up to, Trumps? I asked, pondering the possibility of Stew having joined the acting fraternity... A thespian? Naw... Although... If they ever made a British version of the Addams Family... He'd make a perfect thin Pugsly? Yeah, I could definitely see that now.

After they had disappeared inside, me and Trumper wandered up to the single storied building... Carefully mind, they could have popped out anytime. At the front there was no notice on advertising banner that was attached over the door saying what was going on inside. I could hear music now. Maybe it was a musical.

I walked up the steps, Trumper plodded behind me. The heavy front doors were wide open, but there was another set of swing doors just inside, and these were closed and they had no windows inset, so I was unable to see what was going on. I stepped back outside and followed the wall of the building down its length... All windows had aluminium wire protection, so no climbing onto the ledges... Once I had walked the length of the building I turned to check the rear... The back door was open and a man stood, about 20 years old, smoking a cigarette. His Park Drive packet and lighter were in his left hand, and he was leaning like James Dean against the open door, a checked shirt rolled up revealing his biceps.

"Hello mate... What you two up to? Hey, don't let that mutt crap here... I'll be the one tidying it up."

"He's just been, mister... He only has two poo's a day... And so he won't need one 'til bedtime now."

"He can pee, mind... Don't mind him having a slash... " he took a long drag, then held the smoke inside, like he was reluctant to let it go... Then he exhaled it, blowing it through his lips, then with the last remnants, he created three smoke rings, clicking his jaw to pop them out... For a janitor, he was very talented.

"What's going on inside, mister." I asked.

"Dancing... You want to have a go?" he chuckled at this weak joke.

"Dancing... Like Elvis Presley... Or like ballet?"

"No... Dancing like Come Dancing." he laughed again, he certainly was happy at his work.

"No way... " I needed to take a step back with shock at this revelation.

"Yes way... Why?" he pondered my question by looking at his cigarette, studying the burning tip, and then twisting it to look at the filter. I wondered if he was contemplating all the damage this little white stick was doing to him, all the things mum and dad had warned me about.

"Nowt. Just didn't know there was any of that sort of dancing going in Moston." I stepped forward and peeked through the open door.

"If it's on the telly... It's happening somewhere... That's what people do... Always trying to do what famous people do better."

"Can I have a peep... Please." I stared at him... He took another drag on his cig, he closed his eyes as he pulled hard on the cigarette, the embers on the end suddenly glowing bright orange and white and I could almost hear the paper crackle as it burnt down faster.

"Go on... Don't make any noise... That dog doesn't bark does it?" he pointed the cigarette at Trumper.

"Trumper? No... Only if you say biscuits!"

"Woof!" my dog just had injection of adrenaline.

"Clever... Does he do anything else?"

"Not really... If I try and teach him anything, he just looks at me like I'm stupid... Mind you, a lot of people tend do that too!" I admitted reluctantly.

"Hey... You're not alone, kid... Go on... Five minutes, but if that dog does a brown 'egg' I'm gonna wipe your nose in it! Go... no noise... And I haven't seen you!" he nodded at me.

"You have!"

"No... I... Haven't... Seen... You... " he nodded again, I suddenly thought I knew why people looked at him like he was stupid... He simply was.

"Okay...I'm invisible... " I nodded this time, he smiled at me and then looking at his cigarette again before taking the final drag and flicking it away, high and handsome into the air... And expelling the blue smoke with a sighing noise as he did.

He told me to be careful and when I had a good look to exit by the same door, slam it and make sure it was locked, we entered the gloom, the bright sunshine outside meant it was ten seconds or so before my eyes became accustomed to darkness indoors. Once in he silently guided me, pointed at the hanging curtains and then he wandered off to an office on the left, he turned and put his fingers to his pursed lips... I nodded, then edged forward... The slow patter of Trumper's paws following close behind.

Engelbert Humperdinck was singing about wanting the last waltz as my head slipped under the bottom of the red velveteen curtain... Trumper flopped at my side, out of view. On the floor in front of the stage was about a dozen children, dancing, their ages ranging from 6 to 12 years, I would say.

There were only about five boys, four of them looked joyous, obviously the best day of the week, one of them though, stood against the wall without a partner, his arms held behind him. He looked like he had lost a winning Pools coupon, he seemed to be taking a great interest in his shoes. They were very, very shiny, he could probably see his miserable face reflected in them.

I felt sorry for this destitute boy, he was unhappy, but I had this joy of being a party to his sorrow, Shallow? Bad friend? Or just the knowledge that if the roles were reversed Stew would be having serious trouble with his bladder about now.

A large, heavy set woman wandered between the dancers, giving tips, 'chin up... On your toes... Don't grip her hand... Let it rest in yours... Yes... Better' she skipped ever so lightly for her size, Hattie Jacques comes to mind, big and happy, with a sing song voice.

"Stewart... Stewart." she called to my friend on the sidelines, his mum, pushed his slightly. His response was to stutter forward from the push and stop, his head lolloping like he had no real muscle control.

"Go on Stewart... " his mum urged.

"I don't want to, I hate this." he muttered.

"No you don't... Go."

"I think I know if I hate something... Or if I like it." he insisted.

"Here Stewart, pair up with Yvonne... " a slight blonde girl stood at her side smiling encouragingly and bouncing on her heels.

73

I propped my chin on my hands, this was entertainment in its purest... And I had the best seat in the house!!

He walked, head down, in between twirling couples... He'd of been happy to collide with any of them, feign an injury... Or even better get a real one and not have to go to school tomorrow either. But they glided by him beautifully. I'd never imagined Stew having the dance rhythm, but I'll give him due, he always impressed me with his drumstick playing on his leatherette settee and I could listen to him whistle all day... But dance... Nah.

"Here..." 'Hattie' took Stew and shaped him... Arms up... Kicking his feet apart, then guiding Yvonne into him. His face was turning puce now... His bottom lip was jutting out like a mantelpiece as she attached herself to him.

"Now. One, two, three... One, two...no... No... " Stew walked like a robot... That had been turned off... A little like the Tin Man in the Wizard of Oz before the oil can was introduced... His partner looked up at Hattie and shrugged her shoulders.

"What is wrong Stewart? You can enjoy this, you need to give it a chance." she encouraged softly.

"I don't like dancing!" he said.

"Look... Here, dance with me... Roger...Roger... Yes, stop the music, put on Edelweiss... Here, Stewart, arms...good... Feet... Yes... Right." the music started, she explained to him that he must imagine a square under his feet, then she started counting... One, two, three... At the same time stepping her left leg backwards followed by her right foot coming back then sweeping to her right. Then forwards... Step, step... Sweep... One, two, three... This continued for nearly a minute, towards the end Stewart was becoming competent. I even thought I detected a thin lipped, reluctant smile.

Hattie, clapped her hands and smiled, bent down and hugged Stewart who disappeared from view, enveloped in bingo wings and bosom... When she stepped back, he gasped for air.

74

"That... Stewart was wonderful, truly wonderful... The longest journey starts with a single step... And that dear boy, was your first step... The box step... Well done. Right, let's break for some Vimto and biscuits... "

"Woof!" I pulled my head back under the curtain and glared at my panting dog.

"Trumper... Shush." I stood and started creeping back towards the exit.

"Biscuits!" Stew's voice called out, this was immediately followed by another Trumper bark. I grabbed his upper and lower jaws and held them in a vice like grip. Trumper looked at me in confusion, i turned him and headed towards the exit door.

"Trumper... Hammy... ?" Stew called out again. I turned and shook my head at my hound, he remained silent this time...

I could hear a furore on the dance floor, I banged the fire exit bar... Daylight exploded onto my face, blinding me for a second. We escaped into the fresh air, I turned and banged the door closed... Ran to the four foot wall and clambered over it onto Bluestone Road, Trumper tried unsuccessfully to jump over, and I ended up walking on the wall so he could follow me to the front of the building so he could escape...

"Good boy, come on, let's get out of here before Adolf Nureyev finds us... He he." I bent and fastened his lead, then crossed carefully over to Lily Lane, where my primary school sat. Large and imposing, a massive Victorian red brick building towering over us.

"Back there tomorrow, Trumps... I'll be singing 'All Things Bright and Beautiful in there... " I pointed at the upper window at the side of the school. "... Do you want me to sing it to you?... Do you? Do you boy?" I laughed out loud as he got excited by the tone of my voice.

"All things bright 'n beautiful, all creatures great and small...you're one of the great creatures Trumper, he he." I rubbed his head. "All things wise and wonderful...I'm wise and wonderful... Hey... This is our song Trumps... "

"Hamblett... " I heard my name screamed from behind me, I turned, there was Stew in his shiny Patent leather shoes, shaking his fist on the other side of the main road. "... Anyone finds out about this Hammy...and I'll... I'll... "

"Calm down Stew, count to three... One, two, three... I mimicked the steps that Hattie Jacques had inflicted on him... "One... Two... Three... He he... Come on Trumps, time for tea," we ran me laughing, Trumper with his ears bouncing and tongue lolloping out of the right side of his mouth.

"... I'll get my own back, Hammy... Just you wait." he stopped and realised he was drawing an awful lot of unwanted attention to his dance attire, and Brylcreemed down hair... He turned, and stuck his chin into his chest... Walked like the Tin Man again, straight legged, firm back and swinging arms back into Dunstan's Hall.

The music had just started again, ironically it was Martha and the Vandellas...'Dancing in the Street'... Which me and Trumper were, whilst Stewart most certainly wasn't!

He was probably humming a different tune of they had released ... 'Nowhere to Run to... Nowhere to Hide!'

## VIKING HELL

The music began filtering through to my mother in the kitchen indicating the end of the movie, mum looked up from her ironing and decided she would soon be able to return to the living room. The Vikings was not a film she had any interest in whatsoever... Not that the ironing enthralled her, it was just something that wouldn't do itself... And if she had to do it, better when there was a Scandinavian blood fest than Coronation Street.

"Derr derrrrrr da... Derr derrrrrr da... Da da da da da daaaaa..." my version of the Viking cow horn call was not as impressive as the theme tune... And it was slightly higher in pitch. I pulled the kitchen door open and launched myself into the cupboard under the stairs, where the shoes and coats were stored.

"Did you enjoy that?" mum asked.

"What?" my voice dulled by the chamber.

"The film, did you enjoy it?" mum's voice was a little louder now and tinged with confusion as to why I wouldn't understand what she was asking about.

"It... Was... Brill..." I yelled back, then throwing one found shoe over my shoulder into the kitchen from my dark recess.

"Hey, careful... You'll break the glass in the door." meaning the door between kitchen and lounge... Lounge was a posh word for tiny room that managed to fit a sofa, chair, small black and white television, radiogram and a set of drawers... Oh... Two adults, 1 child and a scruffy dog... At a push!

"Sorry... " the left shoe came over my other shoulder with slightly less power. Mum tutted... But not loud enough for me to hear. I was on my hands and knees and reversing out in the same position, letting mum see my backside emerging gradually.

"Where are you going? Don't think you're not staying out late, school tomorrow." her question was followed by a statement of fact

"Stew's... Going to see if he wants to play Vikings." mum smiled as she collapsed the ironing board, then squeezed it into the left hand side of the small cubby hole I had just exited.

"That's nice... "

"Don't suppose we've got a helmet with maffisse horns on, have we?" I had my head down, concentrating, watching my fingers carefully as I tied my laces... I had not become completely adept at it just yet.

"Oh yes, I have one in my wardrobe!" mum laughed.

"Do you... ?" lace tying disintegrated as I shot my head upwards.

"Nooooo... Why in high Valhalla, would I own a Viking helmet?" she shot back.

"Why would you say you have? I'm going to start making notes of all the times you and dad take the mickey out of me... It's child brutality, Stew sez...and I could even get a lawyer on you an... Get money when I get older... Cost you and dad have been menkally horrible to me... I could end up damaged... So Stew sez!" I wanted to say 'so there'... But I realised by mum's face she was about to have her say on this matter... 'so there' is only used when you storm out of a room, I had one untied shoe on... And one in my hand it's not a good look.

"Well... Good luck with suing me and your dad... We'll let you have the plastic bathtub... And the black and white television, hey? You can take it to live with...oooh... Wait... Live with who? Mrs Wren, next door? Beattie Dalton? Mrs Neary? Send me a postcard... Or a letter from your solicitor." she hurummmmphed at the end of this sentence... Then proceeded to turn her back and fill the kettle with some pipe rattling cold water.

"I'm just sayin'... That's all... All this sarcarsickness... Can't be good for a young boy like me... I don't wanna end up all sarcarsick with everybody when I grow up... Stew sez... It's the slowest form of laughing... Er... Or something." I started on my laces again.

"Stewart? Is that your lawyer? If he is, you'll end up getting ten years in Albatross!" she said with vocal certainty.

"Alcatraz!" dad shouted from his seat in the next room and burst into a belly laugh, the whistled the Fleetwood Mac recent hit of the same name.

"Keep your big nose out, you know what I meant... " she hated being corrected... Really got under her skin, dad would pay later, I thought.

"You would say that wouldn't you? Try and throw me off the smell! I'm gonna get me shoes on and go out raping and pillaging with Stew... ... "

"I beg your pardon?"

"Have you trumped... He he." I asked to my laces.

"Have I what?" she said indignantly.

"Trumped... You said 'you begged my pardon. That's what dad says when he trumps!" I slowly lifted my head... Her tone said I was on a sticky wicket... I was just unsure what I had done to change her mood... Maybe it was dad correcting her.

"No... I have not... Brian... Who taught you that word?"

"I thought 'fart' was the bad word!"

"It is... Don't say that again either." she was losing it.

"I can't say trump or far...or that other word... What do I say... Pump?" Parp?" these continual word rule changes always left me confused.

"No the word before pillaging... " her folded arms were so tight now, you could see white patches where her fingers were digging into her bicep.

"Ra..." she stopped me with a stare... A stare that would have put the brakes on a bull elephant mid charge.

"Yes... That word... "

"Dad... He asked me am I going out that word and pillaging." dad must have been feeling uncomfortable at this moment.

"Oh... He did... Did he?" she stomped by me... Arms still folded. The partition door was closed behind her... Not before she indicated to me not to come in. It really was pointless... The door was made out of nothing more than papier mache and a sheet of glass... I watched her silhouette as she 'whisper shouted' at my dad... Picking up certain words... 'idiot'... Don't believe you'... Another idiot. Dad... He just kept saying things like sorry... Just joking... But that just made mum retaliate with more irate words... 'clown'... 'brain in gear' I smiled because through the opaque glass I could see mum marching up and down in front of him... Just like Mr Beckett did with me at school. That headmaster of mine really hated me... I don't know why... Mr Roney, my teacher, thought I was funny, but then, Mr Roney liked everybody, he was smashing.

The door opened and mum walked back in, she took a big breath and told me to sit down.

"But mum... It's getting late... I won't..." I sat down... It would be quicker if I zipped my gob.

"Brian. What is the difference between boys and girls?" she stared at me.

"They don't have willies?" I was certain on this.

"No... They don't but I meant... Erm... What else?" my turn to stare.

"... Longer hair... They play with dolls... Erm... They wear skirts... Er... " I was on a roll when mum jumped in.

"Brian, take your sleeve out of your mouth when you are talking, there is no difference... Boys and girls are equal... And that word... That horrible word you used... A word you will not utter again in company. By the way... That word indicates women are beaten... And... Erm... Well treated very badly by men. So when you go pillaging and that word... It means you are going out to hurt women... Is that what you want to do?" my mind was racing over her previous comments... Girls are the same as us!!? Do they have dangly bits or not? Stew had shown me pictures... There was no dangly bits... Definitely, I looked really closely.

"What... Erm... No... I don't want to hurt anybody." I said, hurt by the suggestion that it could be in my makeup.

"I know you don't... But if you use that word it makes it less serious... When you grow up you must always treat girls like they are fragile glass... And... No means no."

"I didn't ask for anything!!!"

"I mean" she took a breath and looked up at the ceiling... "if a girl says no... She means... No!"

"Says no to what? Playing footy?" let me escape this hell.

At this point, I'll be honest... I was at an absolute loss what she was on about, I just wanted to play Vikings, I wanted to 'bags' Tony Curtis... Stew could be Kirk Douglas. What had girls got to do with playing Vikings?

"Marie... Marie... Here... " dad called from the front room, he only ever called mum Marie when he wanted her to calm down or think. Mum walked back in, while I was sat there I heard dad telling her she was blowing the whole thing out of proportion... That I was highly unlikely to go out raping and pillaging at my age. Mum countered saying that word should not be in my vocabulary... But agreeing that she had probably written it on my brain in indelible ink by her actions. It went quiet and then mum walked back in.

"Look Bri... Who is top of your class. You know, the cleverest?" she stared at me, willing me to give her a sensible answer.

"Err... Me or Yvonne from the greengrocers." quizzical look on my face.

"A girl... Girls and boys... Men and women are all equal."

"Yeah... But dads do the hard work... And women... They do shops and teaching. Not hard jobs." her face tightened at my preconceived notions on.

"I wash pots... Clothes... Iron... Cook, I take you to school, I take you to hospital, the dentist, I cook and I make the beds, I hoover and polish, I do the shopping and clean the windows, I donkey the front doorstep... Your dad drives a lorry!... And drinks beer!"

"Hey... I whitewashed the loo too... " dad piped up. I smiled remembering being splattered by him when in the process.

"... I work hard... Your dad works hard... But it takes two to run a house and family... Can you imagine your dad making your bed? Washing the pots and your underpants?"

"At the same time?"

"What?"

"Washing the pots and my undies in the same bowl... He he"

"Probably. Thinking about it... That's what he would do!" she laughed. "What I am saying is... Too many women are treated rotten by men, they are regarded as slaves and not as equals to men, and sadly they can be hit too... And, Brian, all women should be respected."

"Hey, Dad would never hit you!" I said defensively.

"He bloody wouldn't dare! Mind you, he is a true gentleman. Treat women like your dad does, you won't go far wrong. Thing is, I just hate the idea of someone hearing you say that word. If I heard a child say it, I would be appalled."

"Mum, you're not going to burn your bra like the women on the news, are you?" the worry showed on my young face... Mum a women's libber!

"Noooooo... I haven't got enough bras to be able to burn one... Ha ha." she started giggling.

"Flipping 'eck, was getting worried then" I blew air out of my inflated cheeks in relief. "... Can I go out mum? If I promise to never say that word." I was worn down by mums equality address.

"Yes" she knelt down and tied my loose shoelace, then put on the other shoe and repeated. I looked at the top of her head, her dark hair, I put my hand out and stroked it, softly, feeling the hairspray, sticky, and I rubbed my hand on my jumper.

"I know how hard you work, mum, making fires, all our smashing teas and things... When I grow up, if I win the pools I'll buy a big house and get you a servant, so you don't have to do anything." mum looked, cupped my face and leant in to kiss my cheek.

"I'll have the house, but I love making a house a home. I don't mind doing all of this, as long as I am not taken for granted."

"Well, I'll buy you a new washing machine and... Err... " mum smiled and stood, before I could continue she interrupted me.

"Go out, go on, it's going to be dark soon... And I want to watch Corra... " she lifted me from the chair, hugged and patted my backside towards the front door. As I entered the living room I turned to dad.

"You should make mum a cup of tea, dad, she's been working hard while we've just been watching telly." dad jumped up immediately, groaning from his stiff muscles, I looked at mum and gave her an enormous wink.

"Good idea, sit down Nod, I'll put the kettle on... I think you can have a couple of biscuits, too." dad said.

"And I'm having your chair too." mum said has she walked to his vacated seat. .

"Be warned... I have trumped on there... Twice!" Dad roared with laughter after he said it, I giggled at his statement and the fact trump was back in my vocabulary.

"You dirty... Good god, I'm surrounded by heathens." mum exclaimed.

"I'm going out, see you later... "

"Forty five minutes, no more, you've school tomorrow." mum said as she patted down the seat cushion. "... Don't have me come looking for you."

"Send dad to get me, he's done nothing all night! Hehe." I pulled down the metal Yale latch, used it to reveal a darkening sky, cold air flooded over my face, I leapt down onto the flagstones outside and pulled the door closed behind me with a loud bang. Oooh, mum will be moaning at that.

I looked up, Stew was already on his way down to me, I waved, before mobile phones, we were able to rely on a friend's intuitivity... We both knew when to get out and play.

"Bags Tony Curtis"... Stewart screamed from thirty yards away. Noooo. I came to a dismayed halt.

"Blinkin' eck" slow coach Hamblett, again, I thought to myself. Stew already had an eye patch on and a sword in his left hand, the 'amputated' right hand hidden up his sleeve. He was always one step ahead. Bugger.

## NANA KNOWS BEST

Nana's house had three floors. I was actually born on the second floor back when mum and dad lived there in the early sixties. It had a back garden with a brick built shed, and a five foot wall on the left leading off it, there was small gaps in the brickwork which aided climbing. Each time we returned and the weather allowed I climbed then straddled the wall, inching along to the sheds concrete roof. Once I was there I was able to see into my nana's bedroom or lie flat and see into the living room through the back door below me.

"You be careful up there, Brian." mum said looking up at me from the sofa, cup in hand.

"He'll be fine, Marie, boys need to be boys." nana calmed her, she was mirroring her, steaming tea and using both hands to cradle her cup.

"Nana... Is there anything to eat?" I called down.

"Now, why would you go out, climb a wall, traverse the top of the wall, spread yourself out on the roof of the shed like a wet lettuce leaf... Then decide you are hungry?" mum asked with a grimace.

"Well, doing all that climbing... Like what you said... Well, that made me hungry!" I explained.

"I'll do you a sandwich... Beef and tomato. Okay? Nana said...

"Yes... Lovely, but not the tomato...don't like tomato!"

"You can have the tomato... It's good for a growing boy" she explained, and I never argued back with my nana, ever.

"Yeah, alright." I'd throw it like a small red frisbee if she let me eat it outside.

"Come down to eat it, you're not eating on the shed roof." I promptly agreed and thoughts of flying tomatoes evaporated, so I began my descent.

"I'll do it mum... " my mother offered. "... Where's the beef?" she asked standing up and placing her cup on the small table that sat between their knees.

I had climbed down on the outside of the shed onto the strip of grass that ran along the side of number 1 Harding Street, on Tutbury Street. I walked up a few yards and turned right onto the little path that ran down the backs of the Harding Street, leading to the shops a few hundred yards down.

I turned right at the first gate and re-entered my grandparents' garden, I leapt down the three steps and when I landed I fell forward onto my hands, there was no pain and a quick look and a wipe of the hands down my shorts removed any residual stinging.

I pushed both hands into the pockets in the shorts and strutted in through the open door.

"Is it done, nana?" I asked while looking at the empty table.

"Your mum's making it... " she pointed her cup towards the tiny kitchen that looked out onto Harding Street. "Go and wash your hands upstairs... Go on."

I exited the living room and raced up the stairs to the first floor, walked back along the landing and opened the bathroom door. There was another floor, where I had popped out of my screaming mother a decade earlier, where another bathroom and toilet sat, but there was a haunted feeling to that upper floor and none of the children would ever be found up there playing alone.

After my quick hand wash I rushed out, and after a cursory glance up the stairs to the upper floor, expecting to see a ghost with its head under its arm, I bounded towards the stairs that lead back down to my sandwich.

"You are noisy, Brian... " nana said as I entered the living room.

"Sorry, nana, its not my fault, I've got heavy feet."

"There's your sandwich." mum informed me. I smiled back at her.

"Thank you, ooh, can I have a drink too, nana? Mum never puts enough butter on me butties and they are always a bit dry... " mum glared at me. "... But they are still smashing, with a glass of dandelion and burdock!" mum received my best 'I'm sorry' smile... She shook her head, she must have had the strongest neck muscles in the world because she was always doing it.

"Pour your own." nana said then mum and her got back to their gossiping.

Into the kitchen I went, the pop was hidden under the sink behind a small floral curtain and once I had pulled that back it revealed the coloured liquids held in the thick bottles. The top was a heavy black stopper with sharp, serrated edges. When you tried twisting it out, it always managed to remove the top two layers of skin from inside your thumb and forefinger... And with each twist there was a squeak or squeal as the rubber on the stopper was inched out of the bottle... I always found the bottle was best placed between my thighs, the neck held with my left hand and the stopper twisted and pulled with my stronger right.

The 'pop' on the successful removal was almost as satisfying as the first slurp, as long as it didn't explode like Vesuvius all over the kitchen. We were okay today, the cork was pulled and the liquid stayed in the bottle. I laid the glass down on the small preparation surface next to the sink and took a cheeky swig before pouring the dark brown fluid, with a mixture of glugging and fizzing noises, it rose towards the top. Two hands were needed to hold the heavy bottle, chinking when it bounced on the edge of the glass, my tongue gripped between my lips in concentration.

Once poured the bottle was placed on the kitchen linoleum, the black stopper was replaced, first a sharp downward twist to get it back into the opening, then a harsh bang with the palm to ram it home, and another red mark on my right hand... Drinking my nana's pop left you with scars!

Dandelion and burdock returned, tiny curtain pulled back to hide it, I walked back to the large dining table next to the large window that looked out on to the back garden.

"You put everything away?" nana asked.

"Yeah, nana." I smiled, picked up the white sandwich, mum had cut it into two flipping triangles, posh style to impress her mum, but always more difficult to eat and hold.

I managed to negotiate the sharp edge side of the sandwich into the open chasm that was my mouth, I clamped down only just managing to miss gnawing off two fingers on my right hand... The sandwich was pulled away... While I chewed, nanas beef was always gorgeous but it was one of the few foods I actually used my teeth and jaws more than three times... While I masticated fully I stared at the remains in my grip as I analysed my next point of attack, twisting the angle slightly so I could get maximum bite.

Within a second of the food entering my gullet beef, bread... And brown HP sauce was back between my incisors, being pulled and bitten.

"Slow down, Brian... Let the first mouthful hit your stomach before you jam it back in your mouth... " nana said to me."

"There's no filling the boy... I'm sure he's got a tapeworm... Or two!" mum had swung round to her mother after her comment.

"Oh, give me a boy who eats, Marie, I hate waste... And look at him... " the both turned and stared. Brown sauce on my fingers, nose and top lip... Tomato hanging from the bread and my head now below the sandwich as I chewed... Like a fireman waiting to save someone hanging from the ledge of a burning building.

"Elbows!"

I looked round, I must have looked like Quasimodo at feeding time, face and back bent as I glanced sideways before following mums orders.

"Brian... " what now... ? I thought. "... Where's your drink?" I panicked, it was not on the table... The ghost!!!!

"It was here a second ago!" I exclaimed.

"Are you sure?" asked nana, which was now bent backwards, her head over the back of the couch and looking into the kitchen.

"Yes, it was... " I took one hand off my butty to indicate towards one of nana's picturesque coasters in front of me.

"No... It wasn't... You have left it in the kitchen... " she burst out laughing, her light blue cardigan falling open as the one button that had held it closed popped out as her heaving chest vibrated with laughter.

I jumped down from my chair and ambled back to my drink, doing the walk of shame past mum and gran.

"You'd forget your head if it was bolted on... " mum said.

"I'm not Frankenstein... Not got bolts through me neck, have I? A defensive reply from me.

"Frankenstein was the Doctor, not the monster, the monster was the...err... Well... Monster." mum explained.

"Was he?!" nana asked.

"Yes, it was Dr. Frankenstein and his monster... The monster wasn't called Frankenstein."

"Well, you learn something every day." nana said with a shrug.

"Are you sure? When we play monsters, I'm always Frankenstein... Or I thought I was... So... If I'm Frankenstein... I'm a doctor, not someone with a bolt through his neck?"

"Yes, and that would be a good job for you in the future!" nana suggested.

"What... Building monsters... That would be a brilliant job!"

"NO... Not creating monsters... Saving people from dying, maybe a surgeon." mum jumped in.

"Nahhh... Boring" back to beef and D&B... "(slurp)... I don't want... (Chew... Gasp)... To be one of... (cough... Bread and beef shrapnel explode out of my mouth) those doctors." I watched as the last part of the sandwich approached my opening mouth, then pushed it in, like the last towel into an overfull suitcase.

My gaze turned from food to the two women sat to my left whose eyes had not left me after my declaration that I wasn't going to become a doctor.

"What?"

"Ha, nothing, I think you may be right," nana said to me. Then turned to my mum and declared, "... I'm not sure I'd want him performing surgery on me... Not with them hands!"

"What's wrong with 'em?" I asked incredulously... Looking at them both as I held them up, mmmmm, brown sauce, I started sucking on each and every brown stained digit, careful to leave no evidence.

"I know what you mean mum... He's not exactly going to be the next Christian Barnhard!"

"Who's Chrispian Barnyard?" I managed to get out before digging a nail into my teeth to release a jammed piece of bovine meat.

"Nope… We'll find him a good job on a building site I think.

## HEROES

"Can we play Kerplunk, mum? Hey, can we, huh, hey…just a quick game… Huh… Pleeeease?"

"Okay, shush… One quick game, on the kitchen table… And you set it up. The noise of them marbles dropping into the tube gives me a migraine." she answered reluctantly.

"A your graine… What's that, when it's at home?" I looked up from the settee I was lay on.

"It's an M.I. graine… It's a really bad headache." she said spelling out the first two letters.

"That's what I said… A your… Graine!!"

"No, it's just called a migraine, for everyone"

"Mum… I think you just like to confuse me, why not just say you get a headache?"

"You're giving me a migraine now… I just don't like the noise of the marbles banging into the tube."

"Oh, I like the noise, it's the best bit! It's bazzin!" I sat up completely now, swinging my legs round and down to the floor.

"Hurry up, set it up, I am not missing Emergency Ward 10."

I raced through the door separating living room and kitchen, Trumper my faithful hound, following fast behind me.

"Come on Trump, you're gonna love Kerplunk!"

While mum gently rubbed her temples with her forefingers, I got the box out of the coat cupboard that was under the stairs, and laid it on the table.

Out came the tube, I fitted it into the tray with the four positions for the marbles to fall into. Then began the tortuous insertion of the multi coloured plastic toothpicks, only the knowledge that laughter and screaming were coming once the game was set up kept me focussed.

Trumper was stood on his hind legs, his feet on my chair, and he looked on in awe... Or more probably... In expectation of food. Then the marble bag came out, nothing feels like a bag of marbles, it's like a fluid trapped in the bag, but hard and trying to flow through your fingers constantly.

I lifted the bag to the top of the tube, began feeding the glass balls slowly, trying to restrict the noise. Trumper's face changed, this was something he didn't like and he dropped his feet off my chair and ran, his nails scuttering across the linoleum back to the living room. His exit caused me to turn and to then spill half a dozen of the marbles onto the floor. Once the bag was empty I got on to my knees and hunted down each and every last one and plopped them in the tube, once I had found them all I stood back and stared proudly at my construction.

"MUM... Ready!!" I cried.

"I'm coming, I'm putting the kettle on first, and a few coals on the fire."

"Ok, but be quick." I pleaded.

I watched mum, light the gas on the stove and put the aluminium kettle on the blue-yellow flame, squashing it so it peeked out all round the base, lapping up the sides of the metal. She then moved to top up the dying flames of the fire.

"Mum, did you know any heroes?" I asked.

"... Erm heroes?... Yes, my dad." she replies after a moment's thought.

"Your dad was a hero?!!" I exclaimed, eyes bright, turning in my chair to look at her.

"Yes, Bri, and a real hero at that, not one of your cartoon heroes in tights and a silly cape. He got medals and everything."

"Wooooh... That's cool, mum. What did he do?" I placed my chin on my hand, the elbow resting on the table.

"He went to war, fought against the Germans."

"What, just like dad!??" I asked excitedly.

"Eh? Your dad didn't fight the Germans!!" she looked round from poking the fire and stared in disbelief.

"He said he did, he's even shown me the scar too!"

"That's an appendix scar, Bri, your dad was only 10 when the war was on."

"Crikey... Only 10 years old and fighting the Germans, wow... My dad's a hero too!" I said with a puffed out chest. Wait until Stew hears this!

"No no no... Oh... It doesn't matter... But my dad, now he was a real soldier! One who looked for mines, he saved lots of soldiers' lives by finding bombs that were hidden under the sand, this stopped his army pals from standing on them and getting blown up, he risked his life every day doing this."

The kettle began a low whistle as it approached a boil... And she started the process of brewing her tea... Her cup was retrieved from the living room, washed and dried while I stared into space.

"Flippin eck, mum, that's brave, bet you gave him a big hug when he got back." I said as mum lifted the kettle from the heat.

"He never came back Bri, he was killed!" she didn't look up from pouring the steaming hot water onto the tea leaves.

"NOOO, the Germans killed him!!!" I spun round on my chair to look at her.

"Yes, and I miss him every day... " the milk was added and then a dribble more to get the correct shade of brown.

She stirred then tapped the top of her cup, and walked back to the table, Trumper following her with his eyes, still no food!!

"I bet you do mum, 'cost that's not fair."

"I know, I was only 4 when he died, and I was only 2 when I last saw him, 2 years old Bri, can you remember being 2 years old?" she asked, a certain sadness in her voice.

"Errr, how old was I when we moved here from Nana's?"

"You were 3." she took a careful sip of her hot drink and placed it back on the coaster.

"Well, I don't remember living at Nana's... So I don't remember being 2, at all!"

The Kerplunk had taken a back seat for now... It sat on the table between me and Mum... My chin still resting in my hands, entranced.

"So I don't even remember him fully, he's just a distant memory... " her eyes were focussed over my head on something or someone in the past.

"That sucks, mum, you only have photographs to remember him then?"

"Not even a photograph, all of them gone, it hurts. It's like he never existed Bri, I'd love to see his face again, because everybody needs a dad."

"I don't know what it would be like without my dad, all the fun, tickling, footie, wrestling and I really love it when he scratches me head while he's watching Branded or that program with the cop in a wheelchair... Er"

Mum looked at me again, and a wistful smile came across her face.

"Ironsides!" filling in the missing detective for me. "... And so you need to be good when he's here, he works so hard for us both... I would do anything to see my dad, just once more... Just to get the chance to tell him I love him, just to tell him I miss him, just to tell him he has the proudest daughter in the World!"

There was thirty seconds of silence...

"Fink I will tell dad I love him when he gets in, do you think I should, mum?"

"Don't ever ask if you should say that, to anybody... If you love somebody, it's important that they know you do!"

"Well mum, I love you, loads... And dad... And Trumper... And Nana annnd... Flippin eck, mum... I love loads of people, don't I, way too many!!" My head slumped at the prospect of all the work involved in telling all those wonderful people how much I cared for them.

"You can't love too many, or too much... The more people you love, Bri, the more people can love you back!!"

I sat up, jumped from my chair and walked to my sad mother, my arms out for a hug.

She reciprocated, pulling me up and onto her knee, squeezing me tight.

"Never mind, mum, he's in heaven, waiting for us... And I bet he hugs just as good as you. Can we play Kerplunk now, I don't like being sad?"

"YESSS... " she took a deep breath, heavy and meaningful... "Anyone for a biscuit?"

"Wooof!!!" Trumper bounded from his spot in front of the fire, like a bundle of 200 odd socks tied together, and ran in circles round mum's legs as she walked to the cupboard...

"Ha ha ha... Mum... He knows what we're saying... Ha ha... Biscuit!!"

"Wooof... "

"Biscuit."

"Grrrrrrrr... Woof."

Two happy hearts in our kitchen, and one heavy one...

# Two Adams Apples

Four boys, all diminishing in height from the tallest, walked proudly, no… Excitedly towards the slope on the Diggy, when they reached the incline they slowed. Geoff, the only boy not in grey shorts, shouted…

"Whooah!"

We all stopped. Digger, who was at the very rear, with his head down was the only one not to hear the 'whooah' and he walked head first into the four foot tractor tyre we were all pushing.

"Blinking hell!" he said one hand on the black rubber tyre, the other rubbing his now reddening nose, me and Stew went into a fit of giggles.

"Right, stop messing, this hill is not going to be easy so we need to get focussed. I will count to three and then we'll push all the way to the top… " we nodded, gripping our position on the tyre firmly, ready to turn and push. "One… Two… Three… Heave… "

We all did our bit, Geoff pulling from nearer the front, me, Stew and Digger pushing from the sides and rear. As we got higher, it started to turn left, away from the straight path we had wanted. Geoff, oldest and tallest, attempted to maintain its balance but the turn started becoming a fall…Geoff leapt clear… Diggers hands and arms were raised away from it and it toppled… Right on top of me.

"ARGGGGHHHHH...Marsy... Geritoff... Arghhhhh" I screamed, I'd been pinned to the floor by the the biggest and heaviest tyre on open sale in Western Europe... And it lay heavy across my chest, like Giant Haystacks on World of Sport Wrestling... My head and arms were visible and my little legs kicked like tiny steam hammers in the centre of the tyre... At least proving I wasn't a quadriplagic!.

"Come on, let's get it off him... " Geoff called out.

They all grabbed a piece of black rubber and on Geoff's command lifted. It raised enough for me to scramble clear. I stood, then bent over... For a second I thought I was going to throw up, then I lifted my dark brown, striped jumper, revealing a plump, white tummy and a chest so red that it appeared I had been the victim of a large branding iron.

"God... I think I've busted my ribs... " I declared.

"Stop moaning, you'll live! Come on, let's pull it to the top, they turned a deaf ear to my whining and began to pull on the flattened tyre, slowly but surely they got it to the top, they all collapsed on their backsides on getting there, all breathing heavy... All smiling.

I walked up the slope, dragging the toes of my shoes through the black gravel surface, grey dust foaming around my ankles. I was still rubbing my chest gingerly and my face was tortured from the pain that my mates were totally ignoring.

"Who's going first?" Geoff asked.

"Me... Me... Me... Me... " Stewart begged.

"Well, I'm not, I've already probably broken me chest and probably me heart is damaged too... Dad told me about a man who just dropped dead from a heart thing... And I've probably got that now... And I'll probably drop dead tonight just eating my tea...is anyone listening to me?" I looked at each face, no they weren't listening.

They were concentrating totally on attempting to raise the tyre, and I was just background music.

"Come... On... Hammy... Stop your... Ughhh...whining and help us... Hah... Get it up you mard git." Geoff demanded between his gasps.

"I'm not having it fall on me again... Do I look stupid?"

"You'll look more than stupid if I knock you into next week...get in here... Now!" he sounded serious... So I reluctantly moved in and heaved rubber.

When we had it upright, me and Digger became the brake, stopping it from rolling straight back down the slope, Geoff, looked like the Vitruvian man... Da Vinci's drawing they used on the start of World in Action... He was holding it upright in a star jump stance while Stew slid into position. He sat inside the tyre, the rim either side of his bony backside, legs and feet inside and holding on with his hands... And smiling like an inmate of Broadmoor.

"You'll have to hang on tight, Stew," Geoff said as he moved to hold on at the back of the tyre, leaning back as he took the full weight "... You two, round the back with me." we let go and made our way to the rear, Digger was a having a fit, he was giggling like a schoolgirl.

"Won't he just fall down when he reaches the top?" I asked, gravity would surely have a say in the outcome.

"No, I don't think so... We just need to get it rolling fast enough." Geoff said putting one finger on his lips...in essence, he didn't know and he didn't want me putting any negative thoughts into Stew's head.

I made my 'eek' face and smiled.

"When I count to three again, lads... "

"I think I'm going to wet my pants... Ha ha... " Digger suddenly spat out as he grabbed at his genitalia with both hands, his legs suddenly crossing.

"You going to have to wait until I've counted to three before you do, you nutter!" Geoff insisted.

"If he pees on me…I'll kill him… And proper dead an' all!" said Stew from the pilot's seat.

"Right, Stew?" Geoff asked.

"I think so… " came the reply as Stew seemed to grab a firmer hold of the tyre.

"Lads, are you ready to push it down the hill?" he asked.

We both confirmed that we were.

"Right, one… " we began rocking the incredibly large rubber tyre. "… Two…" Stew started squealing like a demented mouse. "… And…threeeeee…chocs awayyyyyy" on the forward rock we wheeled it forward, Geoff pushed with all his might, me and Digger at the sides… And it rolled, faster than I thought it would. One of Stew's legs suddenly appeared as he reached the zenith, he began to drop, but before the wail could end, the circle had turned and he had dropped back into his seat. The speed now was just enough to keep him pressed into the rim… The screaming as he plunged down the slope was wonderful, when he was upside down his high pitched squeals were now endangering the windows of houses that backed onto the Diggy.

As Stew rolled we ran, trying to keep up, two either side, me at the rear. Digger was still holding his groin with his right hand, giggling, Geoff was also laughing, he loved it when a plan came together… Lots of yeah's… And 'brilliant's' were screamed as it rolled through the first set of goalposts. An elderly man in a trilby, watched open mouthed with his urinating dog, as this 'Catherine Wheel' of screams flew past him. He raised his walking stick in salute as though he'd spotted an old friend.

Over the halfway line and he began slowing, Geoff and Digger began catching him as he slowed, the enormous black tyre was beginning what we would refer to later as the death wobble. Stew now started calling for us to catch him as it slowly slewed first left, then right. His legs were dropping down now each time he reached the top of the turn as there was not enough 'G' force to hold him in place. As he slowed even more his whole body finally folded like a pen knife and he tumbled like washing in the large driers in the Laundromat, limbs popping out desperately trying to finish upright.

Geoff reached him just before the tyre actually fell onto its side, but he was unable to stop it hitting the ground. As I finally approached, breathless, gasping for air, he was offering his hand to the body in the tyre.

Stew's head appeared and he looked dazed... And confused. He stood, fell, stood again and attempted to step out of the tyre, fell again. Digger collapsed to the ground laughing like a drain. Geoff just smiled, hands on hips, and watched as he Stew managed to maintain a standing position, mainly by spreading his arms, tightrope walker style, and wobbling. He tried walking but he just looked like he'd been at my dad's vicious home brew again, zig zagging across the football pitch... Eventually his inner ear calmed and he stood upright and still... Then he turned his head and chortled as he declared...

"That was flippin brilliant!!!"

"Who's next?" Geoff asked, glancing in my direction.

"You are joking. I've got fifteen broken ribs and a damaged heart and lungs!!" my head shaking was so vigorous I nearly had to add broken neck to my list of injuries.

"Digger? Have you wet your pants?" he asked in disgust.

"Only a little... A bit escaped when Stew fell over... It'll dry!" he said wiping at the dark patch around his zip with his jumper sleeve.

"You better go and relieve yourself... No... DIGGER... Not here in the middle of the pitch...for God's sake" Geoff walked over and persuaded him to zip back up. "... Over there in the garages!" he pointed away to the touchline where ten or so ramshackle garages stood... I say stood, they actually had the appearance of a minute Brazilian favela, the slum houses of South America! There was little integrity to their build and each one was made differently... Both in shape and material.

"Well... I think I'm too big." Geoff tried to sound disappointed, but really didn't carry it off.

"I'll go again... You don't know what you're missing!" Stew volunteered... Oh Stew, we knew what we were missing and that's why he got two more goes. Digger did actually get inside but had to stop before we released him as he thought his bladder was playing up again and the thought of spinning a wheel of urine across the course lost volunteers to push him.

Stewart finally retired after his third attempt. We had managed to roll him at the speed of sound, straight into the actual goal post... The post bent forward several degrees from the impact and they stayed like that until the pitch had houses built on them several years later. But more memorably, he managed to have both legs fall down and outside as he collided...he flew forward inside the tyre, his face jammed into the space inside between the rims, and the next point of bodily contact was his newly developed testicles, they had dropped just days before and they were just about to return home! To be honest... They were not recommended as any form of braking system in the introduction pack he received with them!

Stewart's voice didn't break until he was 23 years old due to this injury and even now he has two prominent Adams apples and only one testicle! But hey, he said it was well worth it (said in a falsetto voice, reader!)... So I suppose we can add peripheral brain damage to the injuries he received that day, too... but isn't this is what memories are supposed to made of? Mine are!

## WHAT'S YOURS IS MINE

"What does your dad call a woman?" I asked.

"What?" Stew looked at me like I was a bad taste in his mouth.

"I heard my dad calling 'em birds!"

"Oh, yeah, birds... All men call 'em that."

"Do they, Why?"

"Errr... Cos... Erm... Birds lay eggs... Yeah... And women lay babies!." he said trying to convince himself first by the sounds of it.

"So... " I scratched my head, nits and confusion, terrible mix! "Cos men don't have babies and men birds don't lay eggs... They call ladies... Birds?" I looked puzzled. "So... What are men birds called?"

"Men birds are called cocks!" he looked at me as if I should have realised that.

"Oh yeah, sometimes my dad says to me... 'morning, cock,'... You know loads, you do, Stew!"

Stew smiled a smug smile of confirmation.

"Knock, knock... " I said suddenly.

"Who's there... ?" Stew didn't bother turning to me, he just lay back onto the pavement, my ball behind his head.

"Doctor!"

"Doctor... Who?" no emotion in his tone, totally deadpan, like asking was a chore.

"Ha ha... Yeah... I'm Doctor Who" I burst out laughing.

"What... It's not funny, Hammy!" he looked round at me now, his face contorted in exaggerated confusion.

"Course it is... Doctor Who... I'm Doctor Who at your door!" I tried to explain my joke, and you NEVER explain a joke.

"But... You're just not Dr. Who... You're Hammy!" he had less problem explaining why it was not funny.

"I... Know... But it's a knock knock joke... That's how they work. It's just funny."

"Well I don't get it... It's like me saying I'm Bobby Charlton... " his hand grabbed his hair and pulled it skywards, showing he wasn't balding... "but I'm obviously not!" this was the moment Stew killed the 'knock knock' joke for me, I would never tell another! It was now his turn to turn the conversation on its head.

"You know that advert... The Milky Way one? The treat you can eat without spoiling your appetite, I don't think there's any treats that would spoil my appetite. I'm not going to leave any of my chips just cost I've had a Mars bar... Or a Marathon. It's a daft advert... And they shouldn't be able to make statements like that, it's wrong, I may sue 'em for wrongful... Erm... Advertising...bet I could get a bomb of money off 'em, too!"

"Yep, you are right, chocolate's great but it's not going to stop me eating my chips, and if it did my mum would think I'd gone bonkers!" I closed my eyes momentarily and imagined chocolate coated french fries, solving the problem instantly... Then Stew interrupted again.

"Favourite telly tune, Hammy?"

"White Horses... " I replied just as quick.

"But that's a girl's song... Ha ha" he took the football and bounced it off the back of my head.

"Is it 'eck!" I said angrily, rubbing my head as I answered him.

104

"I think you're turning into a bird... You even dress like one!" pointing at my lilac t-shirt.

"Arhhh shuttit, you're a total stupid 'biz' head sometimes." my head didn't hurt, but feelings did.

"Yeah, I may be stupid... But I could just listen at school and learn things, whereas you're still going be a girl!"

My face brightened up to a cherry red. Not happy at how this conversation was going at all. Stew dipped his finger in his mouth and touched my cheek.

"Tzzzzzzzzt!" he made it sound like a damp finger on a steam iron. "Trevor Cherry... Ha ha!" I pulled away in anger.

"Okay, big head, what's your favourite tune?" let's see if I could catch him out.

"Oh loads... 'Stingray, Garrison's Guerrillas, Branded, The Avengers... Mmm... Emma Peel, now she's really fit... Gilligan's Island... There's just tons of 'em... But no girly ones!"

I'd had enough, it was time for the silent treatment. We'd been sat on this kerb on Brendon Avenue for half hour after playing football, five and in, we'd been taking it in turns to be goalkeeper until the outfield player had scored five goals. Half hour was enough for me and my thin skin, i was ready to leave.

"Have you seen them kerknocker things?" Stew asked a moment later, stopping my exit.

"What!!" I thought he may have been alluding to the boy boobs I'd recently started sprouting.

"Kerknockers... Two balls on a string, you knock 'em together." he bounced his right arm up and down to illustrate the toy.

"Oh yeah, Alan Moore's got some... Now he's more girly than me!"

"Yeah... He is, actually. He actually does look like a puff!"

"Yeah... But he's not, he's been kissing Karen Simpson, out of our class!" I said with a tinge of jealousy.

"Maybe, but he still looks like a girl!" Stew insisted.

"His dog keeps jumping up at me, wrapping his legs round me, and humping me... It's horrible" I spat on the road in front of me as if the thought had left a bad taste in my mouth.

"See... His dogs a puff too... He should be doing that to girl dogs. Not to you!"

"Yeah... A puff dog!" saving this to my memory to use next time it mounted me. "Hey... What time is it? I'm supposed to be back for my tea!" a gentle panic suddenly washing over me as I stood.

"Not got a clue, but I bet my tea is ready too." he threw the ball to me, too hard, I attempted to catch it but it bounced out of my arms and up and into my nose.

"You dork!" I said as I rubbed at my tingling nostrils...

"It's not my fault you can't catch... Har har... Come on lets go." he suddenly started sprinting across Brendon Avenue, no thought for traffic, down onto Lakin Street where we both lived, I followed, ball under one arm and at a slower pace.

"See yor... " he cried out over his shoulder as he reached his house on the left.

"Yeah... See yor" I made my way over to the right hand pavement and my gallop slowed to a trot.

I reached home and began knocking. I saw my mum's silhouette through the pebble bumped glass, she opened it and I burst in under her arm.

"I'M HOME...!!"

"Give over!" she said lacing the statement with sarcasm... "... And where have you been 'til now?" pointing at her watchless wrist.

"What's wrong with your arm?" she just continued staring at me. "Ohhh... The time... Erm... I've been playing footy with Stew... I think I told you." I wondered for a second if she'd lost her memory.

"And I told you to be in by 5.30... It's ten past six!"

"I haven't got a watch have I? If you bought me one I'd never be late! It's cloudy, too, so even if I was an Injun I wouldn't be able tell the time by the sun!" arms outstretched, she was lucky I got home on the same day, in reality.

She looked at me, frustration was beginning to well up.

"Come here... Let me get them shoes off."

I sat down as she attempted to de-shoe me, complaints from her about the state of them, I just stared at the top of her head, smiling. Did I know how much they cost? I had no respect for the clothes or shoes that I had bought for me, I left them all over the house, never putting them in their place. This vitriol flowed as she was bent down trying, unsuccessfully, to untie the knots in my laces. I paid little attention to her complaints, I heard them on a daily basis. Eventually she just pulled the shoes off in frustration.

"You're getting slip ons next time!" she said as she placed them in the cupboard under the stairs. "Right, your tea is on the kitchen table, and it's probably cold, serve you right, too!"

"I actually like cold food mam, you can eat it faster!!"

"It's not a race, why not try chewing it or, God forbid, tasting it, you may actually enjoy it... Go on... Wash your hands." she flopped into the armchair and puffed out her cheeks.

I stood up and headed towards where the sink and tea were, my dad suddenly appeared in the doorway coming the other way, out of the kitchen, he guided me to one side  as our paths crossed...

"Hello son, you okay?" he asked.

"Hi dad... Yeah, I'm alright"

He started talking to mum while I went in search of food. It seems my dad had mislaid his wallet and was nipping out to his lorry parked at the side of our house on Rudd Street. Mum told him to hurry up before his food went cold too.

I heard the front door open and a minute or two I heard him re-enter, closing the door and putting the latch on.

"It was in the cab, thank God." his relieved voice getting clearer as he approached the kitchen.

"HEYYYYY... What the bloody hell do you think you're doing??" I looked round to see him stood frozen in the doorway.

"What?" I looked up wide eyed at his angry face.

"THAT'S MY BLOODY STEAK!!!" he said, pointing at the sandwich I gripped tightly with both hands, it was an inch from my open mouth...

"Oh, I thought it was mine!" I continued looking at him as I took a huge bite at the sandwich... Tugging it left then right as I pulled on the butty trying to tear a chunk out of the steak.

"Put it down... That's yours over there... " he waved in the direction of a plate of spaghetti on toast that sat alone across from me.

"... The spaghetti hoops are MINE? I asked... Real surprise.

"Yes... Not the steak, double egg and chips... And look at my bloody chips... Drowning in tomato sauce."

"But I like tomato sauce!" I explained to him, as I went to take another bite.

"Will you stop eating my steak... Just put it down... I was only out two minutes, and you've eaten half my bloody tea!" he scratched his forehead in disbelief.

"But no one said which one was mine, and I'm not Kreskin, am I?" I reluctantly laid the sandwich down as I pushed my chair back, I placed it down like I was laying a family to rest, real dismay at my loss.

"I'll give you flaming Kreskin... Eating my steak... Get over there, eat your own flaming tea... In fact, give me a piece of your toast... You owe me that much at least." he held his hand out in grinning.

"Awww... No chance dad... This is mine... You eat your own tea." I folded a protectionist arm round my plate, smiled a disarming smile etched with tomato sauce, it spread wide like my smile, an orange moustache, all across my top lip.

## GLEED MY GLIPS

"Corrrr, fanks Nana… It's brilliant," my mums mother had pulled a present from her large bag.

I held the ventriloquist dummy in both hands, he was three foot tall, dressed formally in a black suit, a red and white spotted handkerchief was popping out of his top left breast pocket on the dinner jacket. He had a white shirt on that required a good wash in my mum's twin tub and all this was topped off with a black bow tie, there were red socks and black leather shoes.

I inserted my right hand into his chest cavity at the rear, slipped between a slit in his jacket, where a pole enabled me to move his mouth and spin his head. His big red smiling lips and wide eyes on a head that rotated slowly, he was a timber 'Linda Blair' from the Exorcist!

"What's he called?" I stopped staring at the doll and turned to my gran.

"Oh, I don't know, I'm just glad to get him out of the house, to be honest, he scares the hell out of me." Mum had entered the room, Nana lifted her hands to accept the hot cup of tea my mother was handing her.

"Have you said thank you, Brian?" looking down at me.

"Yes, look mum, his mouth moves." the wooden face looking at my mother suddenly chomped wordlessly at her, revealing yellowing white teeth.

"Ooooh, don't do that, Brian... He's got evil eye's" she physically shivered as she spoke.

"No he hasn't mum, he looks bazzin!"

I turned him to Trumper, clapped his mouth open and shut at him, he wagged his tail incredibly slowly, but his eyes could not hide the fear.

"Herro... Tchrumper." his tail stopped wagging suddenly, his whole body actually froze initially, then trepidatiously rose onto all fours and then, in an episodical approach, came in for a smell, once he had reached his face, he acquired his odour in two or three short sniffs, he turned sharply and shuffled to the kitchen, stopping once to look over his left shoulder to check him out once more, then he was gone, Trumper was definitely not a fan.

"Why don't you go and play, Brian, and take your new pal upstairs or in the yard... And DON'T let Stewart touch it, please."

"Okay mum." I stood and started for the kitchen.

"Here Bri." Nana held out four comics, The Dandy, Beezer, Topper and the Beano. Each and every week they arrived with her, and this went on until I was fifteen years old, and I read them, Nana's are brilliant. . "Bri, there's some instructions for the doll, as well."

"Oh, Nana, that's brilliant." I grabbed the comics and instruction sheet, and thanked her again, and with the doll in one arm and the paperwork pressed to my chest I headed to my room.

Once upstairs, I put the comics to one side and started to ponder names for my new toy. I propped him up against my headboard, he was sat on my pillow... And just stared at him... Mmmm let's see... What stood out? His big red lips. His large staring eyes... His head... It was wooden. Aaahhaah... Edward... No... Ed... Wood... Edwood Woodhead... He he... Or what about... ?

"Muuummmm... Muuummm... " I raced in the room, Nana and mum were sat on the settee, bodies turned towards each other, both holding cups with two hands as if warming them, their faces now now staring up at me.

"What's wrong, Brian." mum asked.

"I can't decide whether to call him... Now... Wait for it... Edwood Woodhead or... Dick Wood!" my innocent eyes were staring alternatively at each open mouthed adult. "What do you think... Is he a Edwood... Or... Is he a Dick?"

"I'll be honest Bri. I like Edward!" my mum shot out, looking at my Nana for support.

"Me too, Bri, he's definitely an Edward." the support came instantly, through a hand that covered her mouth, even before mum had fully turned to her.

"Do you not fink he looks like a Dick? I fink he may be a Dick!" I held him in front of me, then turned his wooden visage to them. "Annnd it's easier to say wiv me lips closed... Djick... Gegwood, see"

"No... No... No no no no... Oh no... Er he's an Edward, you could call him... Ed, that's easy enough." a pleading smile spreading slowly across her face...

"Don't fink I can just call him Ed Woodhead... Ed Wood ... Head... Mmm... Not bad actually!"

"Yesss, let's go with that, hey?"

"Gan you get my goat gen... ?" the dolls lips moved up and down intermittently... No synchronisation with the words spoken through my stretched, closed lips.

"Your goat?"

"Yesh Gleeesh, my goat, I'm going to Shtewwsh," my jaw was struggling to stay clamped while I spoke. My Nana's eyes were becoming moist as she suppressed her laughter.

"You're going to Stew's?... And you want your coat on?" mum's head nodding slowly as tried to translate this speech impediment her son had acquired, the wooden headed chap had clattered his jaws constantly as I spoke through lips that tried to stay closed...but failed dismally.

"Thatsshh gright... Me and Gri are going to gray out!" I smiled like a moron who had had several courses of botox too many. Face frozen... Apart... Ironically from my lips, jaw and voice box, that slid and bobbed with each word. "Mum... Don't look at me, Ed's talking... Look at him!" I insisted.

"Oh... Okay," she stood, her arms now folded across her stomach to try and hold the laughter in. She walked to the small coat closet based under the stairs, shaking her head, she pulled out my black duffel coat and held it wide for me to back into. I put down the doll and inserted my arms. She knelt down in front of me and began fastening the wooden toggles, one at a time, from the bottom up.

"It's cold out, do you want your gloves?"

"No fank kew, I want to be able to move his mouth wiv me fingers"

"Oh, you're taking it to Stew's? Now is that really a good idea?... He may burn it... Or blow it up... Or even crucify it... God forbid he tries to make a parachute for it!!" shaking her head at the endless possibilities.

"Mummm... Why do fink Stew is stupid?" my eyes asking the question too.

"Oh... He's not stupid, he's by far, the cleverest boy in Moston." her eyes wide.

"Hey... What about me?"

"Oh... ," she hugged me... "you're nice clever, you'll be a doctor... Or an aeroplane pilot, Stewart will probably be a scientist... " then turned to my Nana and whispered... "... In some Eastern Bloc laboratory creating flying monkeys!" she smiled at her as she whispered it.

"Oh... Like in the Wizard of Oz?" I said to the back of her head.

"What... Hey... Don't you say anything to him... I was just joking... He's lovely, really!" she held me by my shoulders at arm's length, studying my dead pan face to gauge whether I was taking in this plea.

"I won't say anyfink... but... He's not lovely, mum, you've got yer fingers crossed, haven't you? he he... But... If anyone ever did invent flying chimps... I bet it will be Stew, and actually it's a really good idea... "

That big innocent smile was back, my brain was now whirring with images of me and Stew playing on the Diggy, each holding a dog lead, each with a flying monkey hovering over our heads, heaven... I might just mention it to him after all.

I walked to the front door, nice and warmly dressed, with my ventriloquist dummy, its feet trailing on the floor behind me. I raised myself on my tip toes, and unlatched the door.

"Stew'll know what to call him, Edwood or Dick Wood... I can let him help me decide!"

"Oh no, you bloody don't. Here, give me that poor doll, it's not going anywhere near Stewart's eye's today, and he's called Ed Wood... And that's final... Okay... Ed Wood!!!" her eye's burnt with their intensity... Ed Wood it was, Dick was a definite no no.

# IN HOT WATER AGAIN

Its bath time in the Hamblett household, it's the late sixties and there is a boy in deep, hot water. Droplets of condensation are causing rivulets on the small, fogged window as they descend, the air is at 98% humidity, a mix of a rain forest and a 19th Century London fog. Through the mist a voice screams, though this is not a scream of pain, this is the sound of a joyous young boy singing...and he's crucifying a Stevie Wonder song.

"My cherry hamore... Lovely as a summa's dayyyyy,

My cherry hamore... Tasty as a Milky Wayyyyy (then louder),

MY CHERRY HAMORRRRRR... PRETTY LITTLE FING THAT I HADORRRRR

YOUR THE ONLY FING MY HART BEATS FORRR (dropping down again)

Howwa wish that you were my... Yigh... Yigh... Yinnnnnne. (up again)

LA LA LA LA LA LA LA LA LA LA LADDIA... "

A loud banging came on the bathroom door...

"You okay in there... Sounds like you've gotten an awful case of cramps or toothache!"

"I'm singing Dad...I don't sound like I'm in pain!"

"Are you sure that's singing? It really doesn't sound like any singing I've ever heard."

"It's Stevie Wonder... "

"Now, I thought he was blind... Not tone deaf! You actually sound like his cousin, Stevie Blunder" a small laugh follows through the door.

"Never heard of him, Dad, is he good?"

"No, he's flaming awful... Just like you!"

"Ha ha... Now I know you're only joking, because mum says I sound like an angel."

"Course you do son," he mutters out of my earshot, "Hells bloody Angel" then returns to normal volume, "I was just having you on, it's really lovely, I'm going to go for a wee now, and then I'm putting some cotton wool in my ears, your mum's is coming up to dry you in 5 minutes"

"See you later... Ooh... Can I put some more Fairy Liquid in , Dad? The bubbles have gone."

"Just a bit, but no more hot water, or there'll be none left for your mum to wash the pots." I heard the toilet door close and lock soon after.

"Okidoki... La la la la la larrrr... La la la la la laddia" I continued, a dribble of the green viscous liquid, then lots of splashing, a weak, white froth appeared on the water's surface, bubbling up, but dying down so much quicker than the bubbles when the bath water was fresh, this murky grey was not as conducive to bubbles. I looked at the closed door, making sure no parent was watching... Then squeezed a lot more of the Fairy Liquid into grimy water. Lots of splashing again, water going everywhere, the floor was sodden. Then the door opened... I looked round, caught in the act.

"Right... Oh good God, Brian, it looks like there's been a flood in here." her face changing from smile to grimace instantaneously.

"What you talking ab... Oops... Sorry, I didn't mean it." I stopped and apologised when I peered over the edge of the bath at the floor tiles.

"Deary me, as if I didn't have enough to do, buggerlugs." she was shaking her head, a large pan in hand. "Time to wash your hair, menace." she waved the pan in the air.

"Awwww mum, I was playin... " pointing at a single plastic boat, sinking near the taps.

"Sorry, hair wash, and goodness me, you've been in here nearly an hour and look at your face and neck, filthy!!" she reached for the Vosene as she spoke.

"I've washed me face!!"

"You've washed your face!!! Really? Let's try it with some soap and water now, hey?" she picked up the face flannel and Lux.

"I've used soap and water!.." I said backing away, knees rising to my chest.

She placed the flannel over the full face and commenced to a large swirling wipe, that encompassed forehead, nose and chin. Her left hand was on the back of my head forcing me into the soapy washcloth.

"Blerr...stop... Blahhhh...mummmm... " speaking through a face flannel never stopped mum from her cleaning duties. When she finished I hung my tongue out, a gave a little gag from the taste of soap.

"Don't talk while I washing your face, then you do not get soap in your mouth." she poured a dribble of shampoo on my hair, and started to massage it in.

"Not so hard mum... Awww... Mum... Slow down." I complained.

"Should I get your Dad to do it?" her fingers now getting down into my scalp.

"Noooooo... He nearly pulls me head off me body!"

"Well then... Stop whining... Least said, soonest mended, and I can go and watch Coronation Street."

"Muuuum… I've got soap in me eye's… Owww… It's stinging mum… " she passed me the flannel, once she had wet it with cold water.

"There, wipe yourself with that." I opened it fully and spread it over my face, wiping my eyelids for relief. Behind this mask I could hear my mum filling the large pan with water, first cold, then hot to create a warm mix.

"Okay, eyes closed, head back… Come on… Quick now."

I got into position, then waited, anticipation building. Then it started, a dribble at first, then the dam burst… Water cascaded down onto my forehead and hair, the weight of the water pushing my young head backwards even further, the shampoo was successfully rinsed away, I brought my head back up slowly.

"Ha ha ha ha… That was brilliant mum. One more time." I pleaded.

"Just once more, then out… " she did the refill, complained that there was no hot water left, then repeated the process, my hair was left shining and glossy. I used my hands to wipe my face of the excess water, then I swept them, in tandem, across my hair to 'squeegee' my raven locks.

Meanwhile, mum pulled the plug, and the water began to drain away. The bathroom door opened slightly, dad popped his head round the door. I was stood in my birthday suit waiting to be airlifted out of the tub. "Can I just wash my hands… Ooooh… Put that away, please." he laughed as he squeezed into the now crowded bathroom.

I put my hands on my hips and rotated… And started laughing… Mum moved in to hide my dirty dancing with a big, fluffy bath towel, still warm from the airing cupboard.

"Enough of that Elvis!" dad said as mum put the towel went under my armpits, and wrapped me like a tortilla, tight with the entire filling safe inside. I was lifted in one swift heft, I pulled my heels up to my buttocks to clear the baths edge, then dropped them to stand on the flooded floor. Dad exited first and called out.

"Elvis… Please leave the bathroom… Then get in bed"

"I'm not going bed… It's only 7 O'clock!" I shouted to his large, disappearing silhouette.

"He's just teasing, Bri, take no notice."

"He's always doing it… It's not funny, winding me up, I get really stressed, oooh, careful with the towel, Mum, yer pulling me hair, and he finks it's funny, laughing all the time, here mum, me legs are still wet,… Fanks, er, he shouldn't do it… "

"There you go, son, all clean and sparkly, and it's your last day at school tomorrow, then break for Christmas." she said as she combed my hair into a sharp, side parting.

"I know, I can't wait, how long to go?"

"Just six days, then Santa will be here." guiding me with her hands into my bedroom, my pyjamas were laid out. I quickly pulled on some clean, white underpants.

"I hope Santa brings dad somefin' for his sarcarsikness… He he." I started to button up my jacket while mum knelt down to hold the bottoms for me to step into.

"Give over, son, you love him taking the Mickey."

"I flippin well don't, I never laff at him, you two do though… And I bet Trumper does too… but I don't."

"You do! What about when he's pulling Stewart's leg… " she looked me in the eye.

"Errrr… Well that's different… That 'is' funny, and Stew deserves it." mum was now looking down, tying the cord on my jim jams.

"Well then, if you laugh when he tells Stewart his fly is down or asks him can he borrow his Dad's lipstick… You can laugh when he jokes with you." she argued.

"Well… I do laugh… But not while he's looking, I laugh in bed when I'm on my own, when the lights have gone out, but not a lot... Just a little... More of a giggle, really" mum stood, examined me, buttons fastened and cord tied, slippers on. She turned me, smacked me lightly on the bottom and marched me out of the room.

"Right, that's okay then, as long as you can laugh at yourself, you will always be a happy chappy." she promised.

"Well... I don't just want to laugh at meself... I'd just look a little bit mad!" I said as I descended the steep stairs.

"I am starting to think we're all a little mad in this house. Corra now, you can have some milk and toast, if you want" she said from behind me.

"Ohhh brill... Can I have a bit of cheese on... And two pieces?" I didn't look round, I concentrated on each stair, these slippers made walking in a straight line near impossible.

"One piece, a little cheese." I was descending the stairs behind my Mum now.

"Two pieces, no cheese?" I haggled, as I reached the living room door.

"No pieces, no cheese?" she smiled when she said this. I turned, still holding the door handle.

"Nooooo... Look you're doing it now... Ha ha ha... There, see, I'm laffin at meself. I'm mad, you're mad... And Dad's the maddest of us all... He's the maddiest-est person I know... " I finally opened the door into the living room, a warm yellow light flooded all the walls from a roaring fire, the Christmas tree twinkled, its colours lighting up the corner, and Dad sat on his chair, one big leg crossed high over his other, a Newcastle Brown ale nestled in his hand and a big grin on his face.

"Come on, sit in front of the fire, Bri and dry your hair... And who is this you're saying is mad?

"Not me, dad... It's way too near Christmas for me to be calling anybody mad, mad people generally give rubbish presents... You're the sanest man in the World!" behind my back my index and forefinger slowly crossed.

# A TOUCH OF GLASS

It's that time of year again, young boys walking the streets of Moston, in their olive green jumpers and caps, offering to do work for charity... Yes, its Bob A Job week... And the 100th cub scouts are out and about.

"Here you go, Bri... " mum held out a bright square of material, it was my neckerchief, cherry red and still warm from the ironing it had just received.

"Thanks mum," I took it and made a triangle with it, held each end of the longest edges and twirled, leaving a tube of red cotton with a small triangle hanging down. This was lifted over my head and put round my neck like a tie, two equal lengths hanging down on my chest and the small triangle covering the nape of my neck.

"Mum, me woggle?." I looked up to see my mum's hand already offering a small coloured tube... Like an enormous red Hula Hoop, the colour indicated my designated cub group in the 100th, and mine was red.

I inserted both sides of the neckerchief that hung down into the woggle and pulled the tubing up towards my throat, finishing off the iconic look of a cub scout, dark green jumper with a mass of badges attached to it, these confirmed my skills in sewing, fire making, camping and the ability to help old people over a busy road! I had on grey shorts, grey socks that rose to just below my knee, with gaiters to hold them up, these had two green flashes attached to hang down on the outside of the calf, a pair of really shiny black Wayfarer shoes and on my head a matching green cap with slight yellow piping, the bright red neckerchief was the finishing touch that made me look one of Baden Powell's finest.

"How do I look, mum?" I asked, turning to the wall mirror over the fire.

"Wonderful, son, I'm proud of you every time you put your uniform on." she gushed.

A knock came at the front door, I turned and raced to open it.

"It'll be Stew!"

On opening it, I discovered a mini version of me... Stew... Dressed exactly like me.

"Mum, we're going, see you later." I shouted.

"Hello Stewa... " the door banged shut before she could start a conversation, he was my friend... Not hers.

Stewart and me approached Hough's greengrocers on the corner of Lightbowne Road and Rudd Street, a selection of vegetables adorned the window, large white writing on the enormous glass window informed you of the latest price of potatoes and cauliflowers, I glanced up to see if there were any spelling mistakes.

When Stew pushed the door open, there was a small ding of a bell then an overpowering smell of earth and fruit rushed over us, attacking our olfactory senses. They say smell is the sense most in tune with our memory, and if I encounter these smells now, they drag me back, instantaneously, to this place and time... And time travel becomes reality. No time machine required, just a nose!

"Hellowwww... " Stew shouted once we were inside.

A large, balding man popped his head over the counter, he'd been bending down and had been out of view.

"Hello boys, what can I do for you? Couple of pounds of King Edwards?" he smiled.

"Err, no, it's… "

"Got a great deal on carrots today… Have a look." he swept his arm over the counter  to point out the pointed orange vegetables in two boxes sat on our left hand side, next to the swedes. I leant in to see what a good deal looked like. Stewart pulled me back, shaking his head at me.

"No mister, its Bob a Job week, have you got any jobs we can do for a Bob?"

"Arr… Let me see," his eyes scanned his shop, then he clicked his fingers. "I know, Mrs Durante, 239 Lightbowne Road, you can take her box of veg to her house, save me driving up there, actually, there's a couple of small boxes, do you fancy it?

"Yeah, brilliant," Stew looked at me and smiled, "Easy money."

"Yeah mister, fanks." I chimed in.

"Do a good job and I let you wash my van too!" his eyes widened as if to challenge our capabilities.

"We'll do a good job mister, I'm a sixer… And him," his thumb pointed at me over his shoulder, "he's a seconder… " Stew declared proudly, not just cub scouts… A couple of decorated ones.

"Oh, not idiots then?" he smiled.

"My Dad says I'm not a full bob!" I declared, grinning like the fool my dad claimed to be.

"He's only joking mister, he's really clever… " Stew insisted, glancing at me with disdain.

"I'm going to have to take your word for it, aren't I," he sighed and turned towards the door behind the counter, "just don't let me down."

"We won't, we've had no complaints so far… "

"Oh yes? How many jobs have you done, then?" he stopped and looked back at us.

"Er… None!" I spurted out with a sheepish grin.

"None today he means. We did loads yesterday" Stewart stared at me and he suddenly got stranglers hands, both ready to grip my throat. I stared back and whispered.

"Whaaaat?"

"I bet you did!!" doubt reverberated through every word, another slight shake of his head to underline his scepticism.

He disappeared into the back of the shop, the door closed slowly, a large spring at the top of the door doing the work. Stewart turned to me and glared.

"What the flippin 'eck do you think you doing... 'me dad thinks I'm stupid!?'... 'We haven't done any!... ' What's next? 'I fantasise about your daughter?' he growled quietly at me.

"Yvonne's actually quite nice!" Stew interrupted me mid-sentence.

"Noooo... No... Now just keep your gob shut... There's two bob in it for us, but only if you keep your big cake hole shut!" he was waving a clenched fist with one finger sticking up like a wand in front of his mouth, emphasising the need for me to become mute. "Don't say another word... Okay?" he glared again, then pressed the finger against his lips.

"There's not actually two bob in it for us,... It's for the Cubs... For Bob a J... " I stopped as his eyes became in danger of popping out of their sockets."

"Gob... Shut!!" the sound of feet made us both pull our jumpers straight and turn towards the counter again.

"Right boys," the door opened and the Greengrocer re-entered the shop backwards, using his backside to push the door ajar. In his arms were two boxes of fruit and vegetables, he lay the small boxes on the counter one on top of the other. There was a creak as the door crept closed behind him. Stew  re checked his green Cub cap, pulling it tight onto his eyebrows.

"You remember the address?" he asked, not looking up at us. He was scanning the boxes then a list, all smudged with his brown fingerprints, he nodded as he mentally ticked off each item.

Stew glanced at me, I smiled back. His shoulders raised and he shook his head slightly. He hadn't got a clue where we were going.

The greengrocer, stopped scanning and looked round at us.

"Well... ?" he demanded.

"Errr... It's your auntie on Lightbowne Road, isn't it?" Stew muttered, looking at his feet.

"My what? My auntie? What are you blathering on about? You... Smiler" he turned to me. "... Do you remember?" he was looking at me, I looked at Stew, he stared at me. I raised my left hand to shield my mouth from Stew.

"He said I can't talk!" I whispered.

"What the... Just answer me... Do you remember?" he insisted.

"It's Mrs Durante... 238... No... 239 Lightbowne Road mister... "

"There you go... You're not as stupid as your little friend looks... " he handed me the list and I put it in my pocket. I turned to Stew and grinned... Stew was too busy sucking on an imaginary lemon to make eye contact. All his features had contracted into a tiny old man wrinkled version of his face. He was not happy at all.

"Yer Auntie... Tssssk... God help us." the man muttered. Then lifting one box at a time he planted them into our outstretched arms. "And don't go eating the broccoli!" he smiled.

"Urghhh... That's not food mister... It's horrible, might as well eat grass." I said.

"It's good for you... Build your muscles... You," he squeezed Stews bicep. "... you could do with eating ten pounds a day... Ha ha." he said scanning his skeletal body, then he pulled his green cap down even further. "Off you go now."

We wandered to the exit, the greengrocer passing us to pull the door open. Stew had his head tilted right back so he could see where he was going, the cap had partially blinkered him it was so far down over his eyes. Once outside we worked out which way to go by looking at the numbers on the doors, we wouldn't be going far, and the house was on the same side of Lightbowne Road as we were.

Stew stopped and put his box on a wall, once his hands were free he lifted the cap off and mussed his hair then replaced it so the peak pointed at the sky.

"Well he's a flippin cheeky git calling me skinny."

"Yeah, it'll be those legs and bony kneecaps, I bet!" I said to my white Biafran friend.

"Yeah, I may have boney legs, but look at these muscles." he pulled his olive green sleeve up to expose his porcelain skinned bicep, he then clenched his fist and brought up his lower arm to ninety degrees with his upper arm, up popped a large round muscle, a thick blue vein suddenly appeared, running down the centre of it. His face turned a slight puce colour, his bottom lip pushed out, his head tilted slightly backwards. He could easily have passed for Mussolini's anaemic grandson.

"Wow… You look like Popeye!" I said, knowing this would help him get over the slight the green grocer had dealt him.

"Flippin right, Popeye… Without eating the spinach tho, mum made me try it once… It was just like mashed privet leaves." he shook his head as he remembered the taste.

We walked on a few yards, Stew pulling his sleeve down.

"Stew… "

"What?"

"Yer box!" I flicked my head towards the abandoned food behind us.

"Oh flippin eck!" he ran back and picked up the box, then returned in a slow jog to where I was waiting. "Great start, nearly lost half her gear in first twenty yards."

"He he... He's really upset you... "

"No he hasn't... The fat git. What number we at now?" we stared at the doors... "227... This is like taking candy from a baby."

"What's candy?"

"Sweets, toffee's... The Yanks call it candy."

"Ohhhh... Well it's not easy pinching sweets off babies, believe me, they scream like banjo's!"

"S'not banjo's... It's banshee's! Idiot!... Tsssk. The trick with babies is, not to take it all, leave em something to suck on... " he explained.

"You are clever Stew, when it comes to devious, you're the best." I said honestly.

"You'd better believe it." Stew confirmed.

We got to number 239 and walked up the tiny path, the door was painted brown with two long pieces of patterned stained glass either side of a knocker. The door was situated inside a small alcove, recessed from the front wall of the house. I put down my box, and banged lightly on the door. Bent down and lifted the box again... We waited for the door to open. After thirty seconds, Stew looked at me, lifted his eyebrows and tossed his head back slightly indicating it was my fault she hadn't opened the door.

"You knock like a fairy!" he said, putting his box on the path.

"No I don't, that was a good knock."

"Like this!" Stew banged the door, the glass rattled in small frames, he stared through the grimy glass... "Come on missus... " he banged again... Still no answer. He put his hands in his pockets and pulled out a handful of items, a conker, a length of string, a dice and a small penknife in his right hand, in his left he had revealed a golf ball, World Cup coin of Peter Bonetti and a piece of chalk.

"Oooh... Peter Bonetti... Not got him... Is it a swap?" I asked hopefully.

"We can swap later, I need him now!" he put everything back except the silver Esso coin. He lifted it up between thumb and forefinger and rapped it against the glass, it was a lot louder and more insistent... He pressed his nose against the glass and stared through again... Nothing... Then harder... And harder... Then smash... The glass splintered into what appeared to be a thousand tiny shards, coloured glass falling inside and outside the house, like a broken rainbow.

"STEWWWWWWW, whatcha doing?" I cried out.

"OH SUGAR!!!. F... Lay... Ming Nora, I don't believe it!" he had jumped backwards as it smashed and he now stood straight legged, his upper torso bent backwards, arms pulled out.

"That... Was... Not... My... Fault!" he declared, in denial. He passed me Peter Bonetti. "You can have him, now."

"Wasn't it?" I asked gingerly, looking at the coin, my fingerprints all over his embossed face.

"No, the glass was rubbish, it must of been cracked already, probably needed fixing, we've almost certainly done her a favour!"

"O... Kay... But not we, though. You done her the favour all on your own" I said distancing myself from his destructive nature.

Stew put his box in the alcove, then pulled out the chalk.

"Put your box on top of mine." he said, I slowly did as I was told.

Stew was chalking something on the wall inside the alcove, just to the side of the door.

'HEY MIssIS... THIS IS YOOR FRoOT AND VEG. P.S. iT WaS NOT Us THaT BroKE YOOR GLAS. iT WaSENT EVEN BroKEN WHEn We GOT HeRE. HAMMY anD STEW

"There, come on, let's go and get our money, we've earned it!"

"Stew... " I pointed at my name.

"Oh, the chalk ran out. For God's sake, trust me... We are in the clear anyway."

"But... " I tried and failed to rub my name away.

"For God's sake, Shuttit, Hammy... We've a van to wash, come on" he was already back on Lightbowne Road and heading back to the shop.

I pushed my hands in my pocket and my shoulders drooped, in my head I knew there was trouble ahead. Stew began whistling, not a care in his world, this was just a normal day at the office for him.

"Oh Bugger." I muttered.

* * *

The door dinged again as Stew entered the greengrocers, he turned to see me skulking outside, the guilt written in bold letters all over my face.

"Are you coming in, Mona Lot?"

"No, I'll wait here, just get the money and then let's do a runner... " I pleaded.

"NOOOO... It'll be okay, stop stressing." always confident of getting away with murder.

"How can it be okay? The window won't fix itself, you've written my confession on the wall and you want paying for it... It's mad."

"We did what he wanted, now we get our 2 bob, simple."

"Boy's?... " a deep voice came from inside the shop.

"Hello Mr Huff... " Stew greeted him.

"How did it go? All delivered safe and sound?"

"We delivered it Mr Huff... But nobody answered, and the window was broken on her front door when we got there. We were both a bit worried, so we came straight back here" Stew changed his demeanour like a chameleon, from bouncy to distressed in a milli-second.

"Her door is broke?... I'd better down and check on her... She's knocking on a bit." he picked up a coat from beneath the counter, and made for the door, stress showing on his face.

"Do you still want your van washing?" Stew called after him.

"Errm, yes, but you'll have to wait till I get back, PAT... PAT. " he shouted his wife... "listen boys tell her where I've gone, tell her I'll be back as soon as possible."

"Okay... No problem." Stew stood to attention, saluted him with the raised straight arm, three middle fingers at the same height as his ear, doing his Cub Scout duty.

"Right... Back soon... " he stared at Stew for a second and then he started down the main road at a pace.

"Where did that come from? We're worried about her?" I asked incredulously.

"I always think better on me feet, knew I would come up with an idea, I've got you out of a hole and we'll look like heroes too." he puffed his chest out, and grinned the grin of a Pools winner.

"Me... Out of a hole? You are un... Believable... " I stuttered.

"Arthur... Arthur?... " a woman's voice got louder and then she appeared from behind the counter. "Hello boys have you seen my husband?" she asked with a smile.

"He's gone to look at Mrs Youraunties house. It's been broken into and she might be dead!!" Stew calmly explained.

"Oh my God, that sounds... Mrs who??? " her right hand came up to her mouth.

"Mrs Durante." I corrected Stew's version of the woman's name.

"Oh dear, I hope she's alright... " she was stood in the shop doorway and was now looking down Lightbowne Road towards Mrs Durante's house.

"Errrr... Arthur said we could wash his van, and you'd get us some hot water and a sponge... It's Bob a Job week. You get a sticker when we've done it!" he held up a purple lettered sticker at the side of an angelic grin.

"He what... Erm... Right... Okay... Er... Bucket... Sponge... Just watch the shop a second, I'll sort it."

"He said to wait... Why have you gone and said that?"

"Just cutting out the middle man, Hammy, and he did say we could do it... So we may as well get on with it."

"Blimey... Have you ever told the truth?"

"The truth's well over-rated... You stress over everything, let your hair down. Now, let's have a look at the van, see how dirty it is."

We walked round the black van. It was small with two doors at the rear that would allow him to put stock or deliveries inside. The front of the vehicle had the face of Ben Turpin, with big bulbous eyes for headlights.

"We're gonna need a step ladder, or... I could stand on your shoulders to clean the roof."

"You're not standing on my shoulders... That's definitely not happening... "

I stopped and looked round, an unfamiliar noise had caught my attention. There was Billy Owen, the rag and bone king of Moston... Holding a string that was attached to a goat. It was obvious Billy had had a drink... Or two.

"Hi lads, hic, can I have a couple of carrots for my goat, p... P... Please... Hic."

"We don't work here, Mr Owen," I explained. "Is that your goat?" I leant in for a stroke, between the ears and horn of the small white goat.

132

"Yesh, I just bought it off a lad outside the Lightbowne. You can milk 'em you know?"

"No way!!" I cried "You can milk a goat!!?" I bent down to look for the required apparatus on the undercarriage of the happy animal.

"Yip… You can milk 'em, and they eat anything, easiest animal to keep as a pet!" he said in a very happy tone. "I need to take him to my son at the garage, then I'm nipping back to the Lightbowne for a quick pint."

"We can do that for you, Billy… " I snapped my head to the side as soon as he heard this offer, Stew was smiling that scary smile… "It's Bob a Job week… Give us a shilling and we'll pop him up to the garage."

"I'll give you a thripny bit… Get him some carrots and keep the change."

"Deal… " Stew held out a hand for the money and received the string holding the goat. "What's he called, Bill?" he asked as he held out the other hand for the cash.

"I'll be buggered if I know… Only got him five minutes ago."

"We'll call him Buzz after the astronaut. That's a good name for a goat!"

"Sssch… Fine… Bush… I like it… " he slurred.

"Buzz… Not Bush."

"Schwat I said… Bush… Like the ashtro… Norrrt, Bussshh… Hal… Hal drink to that. Anyway, that pint's not gonna order itshelf." he began a slow turn.

"Hey, frepence, Bill!!!" Stew demanded… Hand being pushed towards him.

"Oh aye… " he rummaged in the pockets of a pair of trousers that looked suspiciously like they had been made for someone fatter and longer of leg. His right hand came out with a jangle, he stared at the palm for what seemed an age, I suspected he'd actually fallen asleep for a moment, then his left hand came in and plucked a multi sided bronze coloured coin from the pile of coppers.

"There you go... " his hand moved like a badly manoeuvred crane... One sweep at Stew's hand... Missed. Then another which went wide on the other side. Stew turned his head to me, shaking it with a smile on his face. Third try landed the coin into Stews palm.

"Don't worry Billy, we'll drop him off with your son at the garage as soon as we've finished here. It's the big black one isn't it? Stew said as he tied the goat to the lamp post. Billy wandered back up Lightbowne Road towards the pub in a slight zig zag motion. He stopped and turned again.

"NOOO... My son's big and white, hairy bugger too... " he began heading to the pub again. "... Lazy get... " his voice drifted as he got further away.

"A goat? A flippin goat... That's not Bob a Job!" I said after giving up on Billy's chuntering.

"No... It's not... This money's in our pocket." he smiled as he slipped the coins into his pocket, then patted it, making it jingle amongst the rubbish he carried.

"I'm sure this is illegal... It's just gotta be!" I was out of my depth, and I knew it, because with Stew, I always was.

"Chill man... Everything's just fine."

The door to the shop dinged as it opened, there was Mrs Hough, bucket full of soapy water and two cloths in her hand.

"Here you go lads... Be careful, now, he loves that van." and the bucket was plopped by the driver's door.

"We will missus, do you have some steps, so we can wash the roof?"

"Er... Yes. One second." she disappeared back in the shop momentarily, appearing again with a wooden triangular set of three steps. "These okay?"

"Perfickt... Missus." Stew took them from her, just as the goat bleated loudly.

"Oooh... Whose is that goat?" her face a picture of puzzlement as she spotted the horned creature.

"It's ours... He's called Buzz." Stew gushed.

"Oh, a pet goat. How... Erm... Different." she exclaimed.

"I know... Any chance of a carrot for him?... Please." he begged.

"I think Buzz is a 'she'... " she said slowly.

"Is he? Doesn't matter, Buzz can still be a girl's name, I think."

I was playing conversation tennis, watching Stew and Mrs Hough bat question and answer back and forth... And slowly losing the will to live with this make it up as you go along attitude of his. We now apparently owned the goat, according to him!

"Right, I'll leave you to it then... I'll get your pet a nice big carrot."

"Fanks missus... And if you've got some lemonade, that'll be great." Stew simply outstared the poor woman, she stood no chance against the boy with the big brass neck.

"Erm... Okay, think we might have some orange juice... Will that be okay?"

"Brilliant." he said and turned away, almost dismissively. He looked me in the eye and winked. 10 years old, I thought... And she was like a puppet on his string, poor woman.

We attacked the van, lots of soapy water and scrubbing with the cloths, top first, I lay across the roof, giving it a good clean. Stew had at the headlights and windscreen, any talking had slowly eroded as the work tired us out. The goat had demolished the carrot and was bleating away in what we imagined was a happy state.

"We need fresh water to rinse it down." Stew said.

"I'm flipping knackered, and soaked wet through... " my jumper had dark patches where the water had soaked in.

Stew popped in the shop again with two empty glasses and a bucket, he'd emptied the dirty water away down the grid.

He came back out with clean warm water in the bucket, he aimed it at the van and launched it up and over the van. I suspect it was the scream that let him know that I had been at the back of the van, out of sight, and now utterly drenched.

"You did that on purpose, you idiot." I stood like a drowned rat with water dripping from my whole body.

"No I didn't... I couldn't see you... I'm not Superman with x ray vision, am I?"

"I want to go home, and get changed, get the money and let's go." I begged in a tired voice.

"Okay, van looks good, let's see Mrs Hough for the dosh."

We entered the shop and called out... Mrs Hough came out again.

"All done, lads?" she said softly "Oh my... You're soaked to the bone. Do you want a towel?"

"No, I only live in Lakin, Miss, I'm going home to get changed in a second."

"Okay, how much do I owe you?"

"Well, we did a delivery for Arth... Er Mr Hough and the van... Sooooo... " Stew stuck his tongue out and his eyes moved to the top their sockets as he did the maths.

"Two shillings?" she looked questioningly. "Is that each?"

"Yep, that's brill,, it's for charity... And you get this sticker too... " Stew held out the small purple plastic sticker, made for windows, so people who had hired Cubs would not be bothered by any others that week.

"Okay... Here you go... One ... Two... Three... Four shillings... " she had counted it out into Stew's hand.

"Fanks miss, that's great... See yor." he turned to see my face, full on horror, blood draining right out of my face to my feet.

"What?" he whispered.

"The goat!!!" I answered quietly, when he reached me he looked sideways out of the large window, there, out of Mrs Hough's sight, on top of the black van stood our white goat, string chewed through and hanging loose. She looked at home atop the van as she surveyed the passing traffic on Lightbowne Road with a certain regality.

"Shhhhh... " he hissed at me then turned to Mrs Hough, "any chance of another carrot for Buzz, please?"

"Sure get one from the pile, I'll put this bucket away."

"Fank you... "

He grabbed a large carrot and raced outside. We both looked up at Buzz, she stood proud and bold above our heads, a true mountain goat.

"Here, Buzz." Stew waved the carrot, Buzz followed his arm as he teased her forward, Buzz nibbled thin air as Stew pulled the carrot away, she walked gingerly down the windscreen, then slipping onto the bonnet as she followed the carrot, hungry for the reward, I was just looking at the goat, then the shop, then the goat... Eventually Stew manipulated Buzz into leaping to terra firma.

"Thank God... Look at his roof... It's got muddy footprints on it in it." I squealed.

"Here... " Stew climbed the small foot ladders and wiped as far as he could.

"Boy's, oh you've done my van, well done" Mr Hough was back. "... You two may just have saved Mrs Durante's life!" he said loudly, patting Stew on his head... Making him grimace as the heavy handed man knocked his head down into his neck.

"We have???!" I gasped as Stewart rearranged his cap again.

137

"She'd only gone and fell down the stairs, looks like a broken hip, which is not good on an 83 year old woman. I rang an ambulance and she's on her way to hospital."

"Wow... " said Stew excitedly, "... So we're heroes!"

"I don't think we are Stew... "

"Well, you did the right thing telling me, but what was all that scrawling on the wall in chalk?"

"That was Hammy, he got scared Mr Hough, thought we would get the blame, but I decided to tell you the truth, cost it was the right fing to do" Stew declared, I stood opened mouthed.

"Well done telling the truth lad," he rubbed Stew's cap all over his head, "and... Why have you got a goat?" he asked me in mild shock.

"Err, we're taking it for a walk for someone"

"You too lead very strange lives, don't you?" he smiled.

"We do, cost we do anything for Bob a Job." Stew said like a saint. "... Did I say it was for charity?"

"Yes. Once or twice! But I'm going to pop in to your scout hut and have a word with your Akela, you deserve a pat on the back, the pair of you." Stew moved out of his reach, his pats were bruising!

"We may get another badge, an hero one, that'd be brilliant, wouldn't it Hammy?"

"Should get 'constantly lying and lucky bugger' badges... " I muttered under my breath, feeling like a passenger on Stew's make it up as you go along train.

"Here you go boy's... " he handed me and Stew an apple each from the box on the stand outside the shop.

"Oh... Fanks... Er brilliant... An apple." I said, trying to hide my disgust at the thought of eating fruit.

"Has the wife paid you?" he thumbed his hand towards the shop.

Stew went to say something, but before he could try and squeeze him for more money I piped up...

"Yes Mr Hough... And we'd like to thank you... I need go home and get dried now."

"Okay son, well done the pair of you." he waved as me, Stew and Buzz the goat wandered away.

"An apple... Better pretend you're eating it, he's still looking."

"It's not going anywhere near my mouth." Stew declared.

"Bet Buzz'll eat 'em... That's all fruit is good for... Animals... " I said in disgust.

"Hey... And making money, har har." Stew added.

"You've no shame... At all... " I said as I stared at him.

"No shame in being an 'ero, Hammy, none at all, is there Buzz?"

"Bllllaaaahhhhhh!!" Buzz bleated in agreement!

## FISH AND NO CHIPS

Running across the Diggy was always so much better than running on a simple pavement or them awkward cobbles... 'cos whenever you cantered across its surface, you left a trail of dust billowing up behind you no matter how slow you ran. You still gave any onlookers the impression you were the Roadrunner... ... But in slow motion... And without a beak!

We had been football training after school, I was in my football kit, and this was latest my pride and joy. I remember how my heart filled to overflowing the moment I ripped open that Christmas present... There it lay in all its football glory... Manchester United's third choice kit, and my favourite... Yellow shirt with blue collar... Blue shorts... And yellow socks... And all this in manmade fibres... Wonderful. I don't think I ever loved my parents more than that festive morning last December.

Once I got off the Diggy, running became somewhat more difficult, my metal studs on the bottom of my boots made the pavement on Rudd Street ice-rink-like. I had to change my running style to suit the surface, my arms were out and wide for balance and my legs became more rigid. Less bending at the knees... And I slowed somewhat. When I reached Lakin Street I turned sharp left doing a human hand brake turn, sliding and twisting in one movement... And before I had stopped... I started to run forward again, although it was a second or two before I had gained enough traction to move actually make any progress. Just two doors in and I was home... My hand came up high and banged hard.

"Mum... Mum... (bang bang)... Mum... (bang bang)... Mum... (bang bang)... " through the thick pebble glass a distorted vision of my mother appeared. I stopped attacking the door, mainly because my knuckles were now red raw. The door edged open and a pair of dark chocolate coloured eyes peeped round and stared at me in apparent confusion.

"Who is it?" she asked as she looked down at the mud encrusted boy that stood before her. "No thank you... We had the chimney cleaned last week!" she stated dismissively and immediately began to close the door.

"Mum... Stoppit!!" I pushed against the glass, but she resisted.

"Tell Mr Fagin there was not a pocket or two for you to pick here... On your way you little beggar boy!" she attempted to close the door again.

"Mum... Stop it... I'm freezing... And starving... He he... Let me in!" with a little extra effort I managed to create enough space to squeeze inside. Mum closed the door and turned quickly.

"Stop right there... Do not go in the living room... Boots off... Good God... How do you manage to get so dirty?" her eyes were wide open and she looked aghast.

"What do you mean?" I looked down and observed there was no actual flesh tone visible anywhere on my thighs... "Oh yeah! I don't know?" part of the mud was drying and beginning to flake, I bent down to flick a piece off.

"Do not touch that!" mum moved towards me. "Walk, and walk very slowly through to the kitchen, then into the backyard."

"The yard? You are joking?... Its freezing!"

"Sit on the step and get undressed." she ignored my protestation.

"What nudey undressed?!!" I looked at her worryingly.

141

"No... No, just down to your undies."

"And... What if someone's looking out of their bedroom window... And has a camera... ?" that was all I needed at my age... A News of the World scandal... BOY IN Y FRONT FLASHING SHOCKER!

"Brian... Move... And slowly." So I walked like the Tin Man to the kitchen, on the linoleum next to a roaring fire was the bath... A watery green thing... And plastic to boot! It had steam rising from its soapy surface, beside it was a collection of clothes hung on a maiden, a light mist rose gently from my mums washing as it dried.

"Ooooh, that looks hot." I declared looking at the water.

"It is... There are about twenty kettles in there!" she said this as if I didn't appreciate the effort that went into making a simple bath... And I don't suppose I did... No... No suppose. I definitely didn't.

"Hope it's not too hot." I said as I lifted the latch on the back door.

"Don't think for a moment I'm putting any cold in... I'm not wasting any of that hot water."

"Yes, but you can't boil your son... Just because you don't want to waste hot water. That's child cruelty... I think." I gave her my best look of disdain.

"By the time you have taken your kit off it'll be just right." she promised.

"The problem is mum... You're just right... And my just right are no way near the same." I sat down on the cold step with a groan and an ahhhhh... Lifting my bottom from the cold step three times before letting it rest. "I think I've pulled my hamstring" I said rubbing my calf. "... And dad said I'll get 'hammyroids' sitting on cold steps!"

"Hot bath... Great for hamstring problems... And the bonus is... It cures piles too!" mum turned on a ring on the gas cooker it popped as it ignited, I heard her giggle.

"What's for tea?" I said over my shoulder.

"It's a surprise... "

"Oh... A nice surprise?"

"Depends on if you like broccoli!" she said in a deadpan voice.

"Broccoli... Them tiny tree vegetable things?" I stopped, sock half on... Half off. Leg suspended waiting patiently for me to concentrate again.

"That's the one... " she refused to turn and look at me.

"You can't give me that for me tea... Now that is child cruelty!" my little voice at this point was endangering any glass in close proximity... It was that high pitched it was making dogs bark 2 miles away.

"It's got lots of vitamins in it... And it'll help with your... Er... Food passage!"

"My what?" Food passage... What's that?"

"Your poo... "

"Me poo!!" again I had to stop undressing and look at her, "... Me poo... Passage... I'm sure you make all this stuff up as you go along?"

"Your poo should plop out nicely, one wipe and done... Yours is like clay... And it's all over the inside of your underpants... You're not wiping properly!"

"Mum... I do only wipe once... "

"Yes... But that's not enough for you... You need hosing down after the loo... It would be better if I came in with the yard brush to clean it!"

"Now that's harsh, mum!" I squirmed at the idea of touching my toes while mum attacked my buttocks with the severe bristles of that broom outside in the yard.

"Hurry up. Just get in the bath. I'll put your fish on." mum obviously thinking it was time for subject change.

"Coool... I like fish... Batter or breadcrumbs... Is it from Kiddo's chippy?" I stood up and took an age to lift the yellow shirt from my torso, it caught around my head. "... Mum... Mum... Pull me shirt, I'm all tangled." I heard the clip clop of her slippers on the lino and then a sudden, hard yank. "OOOUCH! Oh... My...Godddd" I rubbed both ears with my sleeve covered hands... My face was distorted with pain and utter disgust.

"Oh, give over... "

"Give over what?... You nearly *delapidated* me ears!" I bent down and put a foot on my shirt and lifted both arms up to extricate my arms and free myself completely. I moved towards the bath

"Socks... Pick 'em up off the backyard floor... And your shorts, while you're at it... Do you expect me to pick up after you forever?"

"Are you in a bad mood?" I asked as I stepped back into the yard.

"I wasn't until you walked in like the monster from the Black Lagoon... With this attitude." she waggled her arm at me as if my attitude was a visible entity.

"MEEE?? I'm fine, and why wouldn't I be? I've had a great game of footy, I scored two great goals and... Oooh... Stuart Henshaw's got the Crystal Palace kit... It looks bazzin, its white... With two thick lines running down... Ones sky blue and the other is like a purple... Do you think... ?" I never got to finish the question.

"I very much doubt it, Brian... Undies!" her hand came out as a disappointment furrow appeared on my forehead.

"I wish we were rich... " I gripped my underwear but stopped. "... Look away... " mum put all her weight on her left leg, left hand on hip and raised her right hand to cover her eyes while I dropped the Y fronts...revealing an alabaster backside, I passed the grimy pants to mum and stepped in the water.

"Oooooh... Flipping eck... That's warm." I lowered myself slowly, hands on the sides of the bath, the plastic bent outwards as it took my heavy load.

"Get in... Once you've covered yourself... It will be lovely."

"I'm in... Ahhhhhh...nooo I'm out again... Wooooooh... It's... Woh... Its red hot... And the fire... Blimey I'm gonna be cooked before the fish!... Was it batter or breadcrumbs, by the way?" I finally asked as I sank slowly beneath the bubbles.

"It's neither!" she said this quickly and my brain struggled to comprehend.

"Er... Not either... How can it be not either? Fish only comes in batter or breadcrumbs... Is it in... Er... Cheese then?" I looked up in hope.

"Cheese??? No... It's just fish."

"Is it in... Cake?... That'd be nice... Someone at school said they had a fishcake... Does that have jam in it?" I smiled and began reclining into the suds... The thought of plain fish being enhanced by strawberry jam... Lush.

"It's just fish and it's just vegetables...no sugar... No cheese... No chips!" she kept her back to me while she worked the food on the stove.

"I don't get you... No chips? Fish always comes with chips!"

"No chips!" she reiterated.

"Well... That's not a... tea... A fish without anything round it... And green stuff... I bet prisoners in Weirdways get better than that... I might die!"

"Weirdways?... It's Strangeways, Brian. And die?... Die from what? Eating good, healthy food?... Hey... Stop splashing, there's water all over the lino... You will probably just be fitter

145

and feel better... And I certainly will... If I don't get undies like this anymore!" she held up my recently divested Y-fronts by thumb and forefinger, a distance from her body. They were chocolate mud coated on the outside and there were streaks of cinnamon varnishing the undercarriage on the inner.

"Mum... Stoppit... I don't do it on purpose, do I?

"Check the toilet paper when you wipe... Don't stop until there's no poo on it... Simple!"

"It's not so simple... " only my face and knees were visible now... "... The lights gone in the bog... Er... Loo... Outside... So you can't see anything, it's too dark, the only way would be to sniff it... And don't think I'm sniffing the paper to see if it's clean... No way!"

"Sniffing your loo paper... Good God... Your brain is the biggest sewer in this house! Right, never mind the toilet... Tsk...start scrubbing your legs and... Everything... That mud won't just evaporate off your body... Unless you want me to scrub you?" No idle threat.

"No... No... No...I need to stand though... You can go out for a minute."

"I'll go and get a towel... Make sure it's all gone... And no tide marks." she insisted.

"Okay... Go... Look at my left side... It's all red from the fire... My skin is like corned beef"

"Ahh yes, but I bet your hamstring feels better though... " she wandered from the room as I lifted myself to standing.

"Hey... It does," rubbing a different calf. "... It's like magic... "

"Use the sponge... I'm going to check you before you dirty a perfectly good, clean towel."

I stood, washed as best I could, mopping at each limb gently, and giving the mud and ingrained dirt no cause for concern. Missing my neck, elbows and any part of my back or buttocks.

"Done, mum… Can I get out?" I called out merrily just five minutes later.

"Let's have a look" she said just as she re-entered the kitchen… "… Good God, Brian, how is it possible to have a bath and actually get out dirtier than you were than when you entered the water? You are a complete enigma!"

"What's an *'hin-higmer?'* I asked, the small sponge hiding my privates quite easily.

"It's something or someone who defies the laws of known logic! She approached aggressively causing me bend to protect the crown jewels.

"Hey, I'm too old to be washed by me mum!" I proclaimed.

"Apparently not old enough… Not when I see that 70% of the football field is still attached to your bloody body… Here… Now give me that sponge."

"No chance… " I was not about to go all naturist at my age.

She walked to the maiden erected behind me, it was draped in an assortment of clothes drying by the now dying fire. She dipped her head in and around the wooden frame, like an inquisitive ferret. Suddenly, as fast as an eagle plucking a leveret from an open field, she swooped and pulled out an off-white face flannel… And it was stiff like cardboard.

"Whatcha doing?" I asked with a quavering voice.

"I'll tell you… I'm going to get you clean… You are not getting out of that water… Look at it… It's like mushroom soup… " she shook her head. "… Not until you are gleaming, clean and sparkly… Come here." she dipped the flannel in the murky bath water, then started on my legs, making me turn like I was on a kebab spit… I waited for her soft, but insistent voice before twisting round a few degrees, revealing more mud covered flesh. She was knelt as she scrubbed, I squealed and complained… I tried to insist that I was clean… It all fell on all too deaf, motherly ears... She strove on. She was standing now and getting stuck into my upper torso.

"Awww, mum, flipping...oooooooh... Eck, that's ticklish... Argghhhh." she was holding my right arm, pulling it tight with one hand and running the darkening flannel up and down, a grip like a vice as she did. My body was glowing like I'd been locked in Windscale and bombarded by atomic waste from some disaster or other.

"Stop your whining, son, soon be over... Other arm." I grabbed the 'fig leaf' sponge with my now gleaming hand and offered her the mucky one. She repeated her scrubbing... I repeated my whinging... but she continued to neglect my pain and suffering.

"You'll feel so much better once you are done. Then you can sit down to a lovely hot meal."

"Why would I feel better for having you torture me? If you were German... You'd of been a brilliant interrogator you'd of got everybody's secrets just by doing, arghhhh... Mum... Stoppit... Me ear, you're gonna pull it off... Arghhhh me neck, stop... Arghhh... Stop... Mum!" she was intent on having a dirt free son, there would be no shame brought on the house of Hamblett. She ploughed on through the tide marks, she wiggled in my ear holes... And then when I thought all was done, I had to endure hair washing. The Vosene was unable to lather up because of the pollution in my hair... She took our biggest pan, filled it from the tap and rinsed her first attempt out... Then on the second go she created an enormous apple green soap ball on my head... She dug hard into my scalp spreading the suds to all areas.

"You need a haircut, Ringo." mumbling more to herself than me.

"Why are you torturing me... Why can't you be nice... I'd had a great day... Scored some great goals and saved a penalty too... And I come home... Rubbish tea... Washed with sandpaper... Threatened with a scalping... Me skins on fire... You used to be a real nice mum... But not so much, now."

"Bend your head over... " she said as she went to the tap again with the enormous pan."... Close your eyes."

"Wooooo... It's cold... It's...wooooo... Muuuuuum... It's freezing!" she had exhausted the little hot water left in the back boiler.

"Keep still... It's going everywhere... Brian... Stand still!" she continued pouring while stepping away from the drenching.

"Huh... Ooorgh... I can't breathe... (gurgle)... Oooorghhhhh!"

"Just stop talking... I'm nearly done...this bit at the back and it's all over... " she promised, I held my breath and felt the goose bumps rise like needles across my thighs and upper arms... It was actually painful on the nape of the neck and that was before the icy water hit.

"I... Am... Actually freezing... Now... Red hot and melting and now the freezing... C.c.c... Cold... I feel like I could shatter into pieces... " I stuttered.

"All done... Here... " she offered up a large white fluffy towel, like a matador, then enveloped my body while I was still stood in the plastic bath. "... Jump... " she lifted me as I leapt, pulling me away from the water. Lift and hug all rolled into one.

Over the next five minutes she performed the same rotisserie actions as she had with the flannel... But this time to dry me... She was slightly gentler... And she almost gained redemption with the talcum powder... White heaven.

"Right, up to your room, all your clothes are on the bed... And your tea will be on the table when you get down." she smacked my bare buttocks on the last syllable.

When I eventually returned to the kitchen I was dressed in clean, soft pyjamas and slippers. I found my mother, pan in hand, bent over removing the bath water, grey and grimy, cascading into the white porcelain sink, the remnants of Vosene and the Fairy liquid creating a weak complete foam that disappeared almost as quickly as it had arose. She glanced up at me... A lock of hair flopping down over her left eye.

"Now... Doesn't that feel better?" she asked, swatting the hair temporarily back into place before it dropped back again

"Considering I've had the top layer of skin removed by a Nazi War criminal... To be honest I don't feel so bad now!" I smiled.

"Tea... On the table, and do not give any to Trumper." who looked round at mum in disgust from his position under my chair, big, grey and hairy... His shiny black nose gleaming.

"Flipping 'eck... Naked fish and green food... I don't think he'd want any!" I said as I looked down forlornly at my plate. I picked up a fork reluctantly... I tried to decide what was least inedible... And eventually plumped for the fish... I scooped up the white flesh and placed it in my mouth, I sucked on it and then chewed... It soon found its way down my gullet. I placed down the fork.

"What's up now?" my mum asked accusingly, hands on hips and looking ready for an argument.

"Nothing... It just needs some flavour!" I picked the glass bottle of Heinz tomato sauce and poured it like a crimson lava flow across all the food, hiding the green of the peas and broccoli, slathering it on the spine of my fish, my eyes relishing every drop. I replaced the lid and picked up my knife and fork, before digging in I turned and smiled at my mother who was biting her lip, desperate to chastise my flagrant overuse of the condiment.

"Now... This is my favourite vegetable, mum... Tomato... Sauce... Lovely... He he!"

# TEA AND NO SYMPATHY

The banging on my mum's front door was incessant, not loud, but like tinnitus, eventually it got to your nerve endings and made life intolerable whilst it lasted, it always stopped as soon as the door opened, and it was always me stood there.

My mother opened the door, and without any acknowledgement, I quickly swept under her arm, head down, kicked one shoe under the radiogram, the other just lay in the middle of the room near my dog, Trumper, who looked up at me with disgust.

"Pick up your shoes Brian and put them in the cupboard, please."

"Awww, mum, can I do it later?"

"Now Brian, please."

"Let me get me breath back, I've just run all the way from the church chapel!"

I was now laid, inverted, upside down on the chair, head balancing on the carpet, feet knocking the antimaccasar over the back of the chair onto the floor.

"Why have you been running?" she asked suspiciously.

"Stew said something horrible to Mrs Neary, she started coming down the path... So I ran, she scares me"

"Brian, I hope you didn't give cheek."

"Nope, never do, I just ran.

The word newsflash appeared in black capitals, on a white rectangle across the bottom of the  screen, followed by a news reader looking and sounding solemn and serious as he spoke.

Striking music accompanied it. Mum turned from me to the black and white screen, pushing ever so gently to one side, she slowly moved to the settee, never taking her eyes from the screen.

"Right, let me watch this newsflash, please" she sat up intently, head forward… Eager for the news.

"Can I have a jam butty please, mum?" I whined.

"Yes, but you'll have to make it yourself,… And make sure you put everything away." she said dismissively… her hand waving me towards the kitchen as she stared deeply at the man on television and the piece of paper he was reading off.

I collapsed onto my head, shoulders and finally rolled onto my knees, no grace, more like a dead body being thrown from a slow moving truck. My own cooking, yesss, freed from my shackles in the kitchen! I raced into the kitchen as the newscaster intoned his boring information… Adults only!!

In the kitchen I placed the bread flat on the blue table, shovelled the soft butter onto the thick white slice, there was enough to cover the entire linoleum on the kitchen floor, my knife delved into the strawberry jam, leaving butter in the jar, mum would not like that… Three times I dipped, I spread the thick and lumpy compote across the buttered bread, the knife, jammy and sticky, was put in my mouth and sucked clean, I kept one eye on the door, again, this could result in an unhappy mum. Once I had inspected the knife, making sure it was clean, it was dumped onto the table, and the buttered slice was raised and unceremoniously slammed onto the jammed slice, palm pushing it down hard, leaving grimy fingerprints in the imprint from my unwashed hand. Jam squelched and ran from the sides of this barely edible monstrosity, and when I picked it up it was heavy and my eyes locked onto it, wide, the gastric juices flooded my mouth.

The table had the look of a drive by shooting... Red everywhere, bar a squarish clean spot where the bread had lain. I walked as I munched back to the living room.

"Stewart eats... Sugar butties... And he likes the crusts off the end of the ... Loaf!" I said between the gaps of my chomping, taking moments to breath in through the small gaps in my mouth that were not solid with bread, butter and jam.

"Does he?" mum's voice was quiet, soft, and not inquisitive at all.

"Yep, it's horrible... And... All the... Crusts, .and he's not got... (gasp)... Any... Curly hair!!!?"

"No?" soft again, I finally looked up from my feast at mum.

"What's wrong mam?" she was sat with her elbows on her knees, a hanky at her mouth.

"Nothing son, think I may be coming down with a cold."

"Do you remember my cold, I had that horrible green snot, it was all over me face... Do you remember... Mum?" she looked round at me, eyes watery, she nodded.

"Aww mam, you look really horrible, should I make you a cup of tea?"

"Oh Bri, that would be lovely... You're a good boy."

"I know, Stews mum wishes he was more like me, she says he's a little devil... She can't find her best cup... We both wee'd in it to see who could wee the most ... I won, two cups full." I said triumphantly.

"Oh did you... ?" she really wasn't listening, so I headed for the kitchen, whistling 'What a Wonderful World' by Louis Armstrong, my dad's favourite record at that moment.

I walked, sandwich in one hand down by side, oozing jam onto my grey shorts, still yammering on about how Stew's mum thought I was wonderful in between my whistles... And the television continued its broadcast.

"... So just to confirm, Senator Robert Kennedy has been pronounced dead after the shooting in Los Angeles, in the kitchens of The Ambassador Hotel... "

"Two sugars mum?" I called from our little kitchen in Manchester, England.

## THE WRONG BROTHERS

The hood of my coat clung to my head, and due to the fact I hadn't buttoned it up or even inserted my arms, the rest was caught in a strong wind that kept the rest of it at 45 degrees, desperately trying to escape my body. I looked to all intents and purposes like a poor mans, cloaked superhero... Duffel Coat Boy!

There we were, Stewart, Trumper and myself walking into 'Mother Nature's' gusts, leaning forwards in an attempt to help our progress up Rudd Street. Trumper's fur looked liable to be torn from his skin at any moment, it lifted and dropped like ten million tiny wings trying their canine platform.

Stew was struggling to contain the object he was carrying, it was almost as tall as him and white material billowed constantly in his hands. He pulled it closer to his body his knuckles white with the effort.

"Perfect day for it... " he said.

"Abso... Flippin... Lutely!" I agreed, shouting above the noise of the incessant flapping of our latest project.

Our stride got shorter as we climbed the slight incline to the Diggy, the wind plus the rise making it even more difficult to walk.

"Nearly there... " I shouted, Stew just nodded, his energy reserves were low now.

Once we had reached then crossed the plateau, we stopped and gazed across the dark cinder plain that lay below us, goalposts just in front of us and another set at the other end of this barren recreational area. I smiled as I envisaged the fun ahead.

"Let's go fly a kite...up to the highest height... " Stew had begun the descent and burst into his best Dick van Dyke accent. "... Up through the atmosphere, up where the air is clear... Oh let's go fly a kite." I couldn't restrain my laughter as Trumper and I followed him down.

The 'kite' was a Stew special, he had supersized the normal format, he then somehow persuaded me to let him hack my mother's yard brush down, leaving her an 18 inch handle. The piece we'd taken was now the cross beam, his mother had no handle at all! He used hers as the central vertical strut and had nailed, screwed and finally used a whole roll of sellotape to secure the two poles together, Stew was a belt and braces and string sort of guy.

"That bed sheet you got from your mums washing basket is just perfect for the job, it was just the right size." he said as he laid the kite on the floor.

"Mustn't of been perfect or you wouldn't have had to cut all that off before." I grimaced at the thought of mum searching high and low for her bed linen.

"It says on here it's Egyptian cotton... So it's probably dead cheap... She'll probably just buy another one for two bob on the market... " he said as he carefully tied the string to the wooden frame, I say string, it was two washing lines from each of our back yards and a roll of garden twine from Stew's granddads all attached together in the strongest knots we could find in our Cubs handbook.

"Mums going to go ballistic, this is bound to be a good drying day!" I pointed up at the clouds scudding across the sky.

"You worry too much... They shout and scream but that's it... They're okay ten minutes later."

"She may be okay ten minutes later, but every time she has to brush the back yard she's going to have to use a brush with an 18 inch handle... "

"She can get Little Dave Marsden in to do her brushing, it'll be the right size for him!"

"I don't think you can use 4 year olds for manual labour anymore, Stew."

"It's not exactly sticking him up a chimbley, is it... Although... "

"You are not pushing Dave up our chimmley, Stewart, his mum is not your biggest fan as it is!"

"Bet it's still the best way to clean one though... And if the boy wants to do it, you shouldn't be able to say you can't, just because of some barmy health and safety law." he argued.

"It's not barmy if young boys aren't getting cooked over a fire, is it?"

"This is how you are, Hammy, safe... No risk... No danger." he tugged on the cord a couple of times to convince himself it was firmly attached and stood back up.

"All done?" I enquired.

"Yep, nearly ready for take-off... Unravel the rest of that twine."

I walked backwards unrolling the ball of hairy string, until I was about twenty five yards away.

"Will this be enough?" I lay the string down and returned to the kite.

"Should be... We don't want to bring down a Jumbo jet do we... Har har... Or do we?" he suddenly went quiet as he thought it through.

"No... We don't is the correct answer, Stew."

"Well, maybe just scare one... ?" he laughed again.

"Most of Moston are going to think it's an enormous U.F.O.! The flipping size of it... He he."

It was time to work out which way the wind was coming from, once this was done we aligned the kite so when Stew lifted it, the wind would gather in the cotton sheet then lift it high into the Mancunian sky.

"I'll start running towards you... At the same time as you are running away from me...you pull on the string over your shoulder, when it lifts up I'll come and help you hold the string... Okay? Understand?" he said slowly.

I followed the line back and lifted it and turned to show Stew.

"Ready when you are Stew!" he waved and bent to pick up the gigantic kite. He struggled a little as the wind tried to launch it prematurely, then he pulled it until the line was tight between us. The kite was the lifted behind his head and several times it threatened to be pulled free.

"Hammy, after three... " I gave him the thumbs up and turned away, ready to run.

"ONE... ... TWO... ... THREEEEEE...RUNNNNN... " he screamed, he held onto the crossbeam and raced towards me.

"Flipping...eck... " I was already out of breath ten yards in.

"YAAAAARGHHHHHHHH!" the scream was behind me and a second later the line I was holding went tight, pulling me to a halt, instantly. I was actually pulled slightly backwards, but the cord was wrapped around my hand so I remained attached.

I spun round to see what the problem was and my brain had difficulty computing the image that appeared on my retinas. Stew was airborne, and getting higher by the second, I attempted to pull him back to Earth while the kite made every effort to pull my arms from their sockets.

"HAMMMY...HAMMMMMMY... Warghhhhhhh..." his screams were glass shatteringly high, not as high as him, but high. He was about twenty five feet off terra firma, both legs were kicking forwards and backwards, like doggy paddle in the clouds.

"I'm trying... To... Get you down!" I pulled as hard as I could again, falling to my backside, Trumper had started barking up at Stew's flailing legs, the scene was becoming manic.

"DON'T WORRY... ... Urghh... I'LL GET YOU...DOWWWN... " the blood was being cut off to my hands now, digging deep into the flesh, my heels were being dragged through the dirt surface, as the high gusts tried to pull him away.

"NOOOOO...I'M JUST...SAYING...I CAN...SEE YOUR HOUSE FROM HERE!!!" he yelled, happiness spilling from every word.

"WHATTT!" suddenly the wind dropped a little, and the kite dropped ten feet, Stew took the opportunity to unwrap his fingers from the wooden strut and he fell... Like a stone. He hit the ground and dust exploded up and they disappeared instantly on a fresh gust of wind.

Trumper reached him first, and began nuzzling into his neck, Stew was laid in the foetal position and was not moving. I raced back towards my two friends, the kite twirled twice and dived like a rocket into the ground ten feet from his head.

I reached his body and fell to my knees by his head, and bent down to see if he was still breathing.

Stew, Stew... You okay," I asked in desperation, "... Stew... Come on." I pulled his shoulder and turned him slightly to one side, his hands were covering his face until one dropped revealing the biggest smile I'd seen in a long time.

"You okay?" I asked as I sat back on my haunches.

"More than alright, Hammy, that was unbelievable..." he rolled onto his back and spread his arms and legs wide...like a giant X "I just flew, Bri, in the sky...I actually flew like a bird!"

"I've always said you looked like a bird... A real cuckoo!" I stood and wiped imaginary dust from my shorts. "... Or a giant tit...or... Erm... Dicky bird... Or a booby... That's a bird you know... He he.

Stew lifted himself into a sitting position and crossed his legs.

"Are you having a go?"

"Now... Me... I'm an emu... Or a penguin... Or an ostrich... " I shook my head and gave out a laugh.

"You, Hammy a total chicken!" he pointed at me. "Get the kite, I'm going up again!" he stood slowly and rubbed his thighs.

"Are you completely mad? You'll end up killing yourself!"

"Hammy, life's for living. Now, you can watch me live mine... And one day I will tell you how much fun I had, while you stood around watching, with your feet on the ground." me and Trumper stood open mouthed at this pioneer of stuntmanship... He was my Mancunian Chuck Yeager.

## LET THE CARDS FALL

"... Got, got, got, not got... Got, got, got, got, not got, got, not got... Oooh... An Alan Ball!!!" I held the football card in my hand and gazed upon with green eyed covetousness, craving ownership. Alan Ball was the left footed, ginger headed midfield genius. He spoke like a castrato and wore the most iconic and impracticable white football boots, and we all thought he was really cool, especially our mate Gary McConnell, who just so happened to be ginger haired and left footed.

"I know, I just got it in a pack from Dave's newsagents" said Stew. "I bought one pack for a penny, and when he turned round I pinched 2 more out of the box on the counter!" he had a big smile and was chewing three sticks of the pink gum from the packs, all sloshing around in his big, happy gob.

We were sat on the pavement on Brendan Avenue, with our backs against the McConnell's wall. The sun was shining and warming us up on a glorious Sunday morning.

"I will swap you a... " I started going through my very large bundle of orange backed 1971 football cards, "... Bobby Charlton and a Harry Redknapp... Errr... Plus a Gordon Banks, if you give me Alan Ball."

"No way, do you think i just got off the idiot bus?, I want at least your Denis Law, Emlyn Hughes, Ian Hutchinson, Johnny Giles annnnd... Your England picture checklist card!"

"No chance, me checklist... Has your brain fell out of your ear?" I looked at Stew like he had lost his mind.

The bartering went on for a few more minutes, with George Eastham's name proposed by me, to no avail. Stewart reached over for my pack.

"Let's have another look... Wagstaffe... Rubbish... Mike England... Not bad... Clyde Best, is he related to George? What you looking at me like that for? Chris Lawler... Alright... Peter Storey... Nope... Wyn Davies... He can head the ball faster than most players can kick, you know?" apparently I didn't.

"Tell you what Hammy, we'll play nearest the wall for it, you throw first, and nearest gets to keep the cards... OK?"

"All right, but only my checklist against your Alan Ball!" he reluctantly agreed and we turned to face the wall. My hand shook a little as I sought out the checklist with the 1970 England team photograph taken in Mexico the previous summer in the World Cup Finals.

I stood with my feet pressed firmly into the kerb, confident, leaning as far forward as possible without falling over onto my face. This stance was similar to the one Eric 'the Crafty Cockney' Bristow would use when he stood at the oche a few years later.

I took the England card and carefully placed it between my middle and my index finger, I slowly pulled my hand back and upwards to my shoulder, then with a graceful, almost balletic sweep, pulled it back down and out in front of me, releasing the card just as the arm reached full arm extension... The card whizzed away from me, spinning like a helicopter blade, fast and orange. It fell forward, low towards the pavement, skimming low across the black tarred surface, then just before the wall it landed, it slid along for a further three inches and just touched the bottom brick, next to the drainpipe. Pure poetry in motion!

"Yessss!!!!" I bounced around, no grace, no sportsmanship...Alan Ball looked like he was about to be transferred.

Stew said nothing, he didn't need to, his face spoke volumes, there was a mini thunderstorm breaking out on his brow.

He moved purposefully to the oche, Alan Ball was in the same position finger wise, as England had been moments before in mine. Stews action was simple, the sweep not quite as theatrical as mine, and when he released Bally, he stumbled through the air, no elegance, no poetry... The flight of a drunken bumble bee, he hit the floor well short of my card, but it tumbled like a man thrown from a motorcycle at 100mph... Head over tail, cartwheeling closer to the brickwork... The card arrived at the wall, stumbled erratically, and finally ended upright, leaning at a 77 degree angle. Un... Bloody... Believable!!!! I nearly fainted away.

"OH YESSSS!!" Stew was euphoric, "... What... A... Throw!" he dropped to his knees and punched the air.

You see, an upright card always trumps a card just touching the wall... It was the universal rule of the standing card... There would be no higher court to go to try and overturn this judgement... I was seeing my country slip from my hands.

"NOOOO!!... You jammy pig, that was a rubbish throw." I squealed like a stuck pig.

But I was already talking to his back, he was lifting my prized England card to his lips, pressing it to his lips like Bobby Moore kissing Jules Rimets trophy in '66. Once he had finished his slobbering he lifted it high and proud.

"What about double or quits?... My Franny Lee... ?" I begged.

"Nope, not losing this baby... Haha... Do you know how rare these are????" Stew was in football card nirvana.

We sat down, Stew looking at the back of the checklist... 171 all the way up to 266... Completely unmarked, I looked sullenly down at it too, from his shoulder…now it was a loved one being pawed by Stewart Neale, my friend… My neighbour and my flaming eternal nemesis… How was I to know at this moment in time that this was not the last occasion that this boy would grip  so many of the things I felt great affection for… Theresa, Geraldine, Shelley… Et al… If I liked it… He took it… But I'm not a bitter guy… I'm not… Honest to God… Nothing crossed!

## MOTHER OF INVENTOR

"Mum, how much do inventors get paid?" the question had come from out the blue.

"Well it all depends on what you invent, it's not a set wage, I don't think" she replied, iron in hand.

"Well, let's see...what did the man who invented telly get paid then?"

"Logie Baird... I don't know. Quite a lot, I expect." she was trying to concentrate on her ironing whilst watching Crossroads.

"Yogi Bear invented television... No way?!!!!."

"John Logie Baird... The famous Scottish inventor... Not the cartoon character. |You Booboo!!" she shook her head in despair.

"Well, actually... Thought it that woulda been rather funny... 'cost he's a bear!"

"... And not real. He's just a cartoon character." she did a little nod towards me, confirming I understood how reality worked.

"Yeah... Of a bear... And bears don't invent things, whereas, Professor Pat Pending on the Wacky Races, he does invent things!"

"Okay... Let's leave it now." she had decided the unwinnable argument needed bringing to a halt.

"Anyway. I've been thinking of things to invent and to be honest it ain't easy." I said with a frown.

"Well if it was easy... Everyone would be at it, wouldn't they?" she replied still staring at the television, her right arm constantly swooshing over crumpled clothes on the ironing board.

"What would make your life easier... What could I invent that you would buy?"

"A robot that would do this pile, I hate ironing.!" she said pointing at a large basket of recently washed clothes.

"Do you... Why?" not understanding how being in charge of red hot iron wouldn't be a continual joy.

"Because it's boring." she answered succinctly.

"But you're watching Coronation Street at the same time... So it can't be that hard."

"Its Crossroads... And I make it look easy, it isn't believe me. Once you've finished, another load of clothes start filling the basket... It's just a vicious circle."

"A vicious circle!!" I liked the sound of that. "A circle that is vicious...grrrr... He he!?" I smiled as I let my imagination roam free... Putting both hands in the claw position near my growling mouth.

"It's a cycle... And before you ask, not a bicycle... " she said as I opened my mouth to leap in with another potty statement. "... That never ends... You get clothes dirty... I wash the clothes... I iron the clothes... You wear the clothes and get them dirty again... See... A never ending circle!" she explained twirling her finger round and round to emphasise this.

"Yeah... But it's not really vicious. It's a little bothersome maybe... Not vicious... It's a bothersome circle.

"Well... It   honestly feels more vicious than just bothersome... And if you had to do it, you'd understand." she said taking her eyes from the telly to give me 'the eyes.'

"Ha, yeah... But I'm not a girl, so I don't ever need to learn, although I might invent clothes that don't need ironing... That'd be good for you, wouldn't it?" I smiled benevolently.

"You may need to learn to iron your shirts one day, son, so maybe it's best you invent clothes that never need ironing. I won't be here forever."

"I'll get Nana to do 'em then."

"Oh... Cos she's going to outlive me!! Thank you! Okay, clever clogs... You just to consider the possibility that you may be living alone when you grow up, and clothes don't iron themselves."

"Trumper will still be living with me... Although he'd be useless ironing."

"Or you could get married... ?" she smiled as she said this.

"Or I could get a butler... Yeah... I'll get a butler like Lurch in the Addams Family... He he."

"Or... You could get married and give me grandchildren... " persisting with the married with kid's line.

"Or... I could just invent something that makes you live forever... " I opened my arms as if I had solved future my ironing issues.

"So, you'd only want me to live for ever just so I can iron your shirts... ?!!" she put the iron down carefully.

"Not just iron, you can and sew my buttons back on... And make me meals... And change me bed... And... " I looked at my potential life maid's face, it was grimacing a little more with each reason I gave, "yeah... And give me hugs... And tuck me in at nights, and you'd be there so I can make a cup of tea for... Hey... Do you fancy a nice cup of tea, mum?" I grinned my most disarming smile.

"Please... Two sugars and leave the tea bag in for more than five seconds... And not half a pint of milk either... And tidy up have yourself, it's never the same if I have to clean the whole kitchen again as the price for a cup of tea"

"Hey, hang on. I'm not your slave... You're mine... He he."

167

## A Cure for the Pox

Rat... Tat... Tat... Tat... Tat... Tat... Rat... Tat... Tat... The sound of the front door being attacked by a young boys knuckles.

"I'm coming, stop the banging, bullet head!" dad called through the thick glass.

rat... Tat... Tat... Rat... Tat... I continued, he really needed to know I wanted to get in.

The door swung open, my Dad stood, one hand holding the lock, the other leaning against the frame, creating a natural arch for me to march through... And today was the death march, a slow, feet dragging, tromp. Face like a wet weekend in Morecambe, behind me, Trumper, bouncing, tail all awag... Obviously, unlike me, trouble free.

"Hello Dad, thanks for opening the door, sorry for banging incessantly on the front door like an insane, 4 foot, giant, death watch beetle... Hey, that's okay son, I quite like being woken from an afternoon nap, in fact, I love it, I find it the most refreshing way to wak... " my dad said in a calm voice until I interrupted.

"Stop being 'sarcarsick,' I am fed up, fed to here." my hand, horizontal, banging it three times on my forehead, a miniature Freddie Parrot Face!!

Dad closed the door, turned and folded his arms, and looked at me sternly.

"Okay, what's he been up to now... It is Stewart again, isn't it?" he asked sympathetically.

"Yep,... " I replied, flicking a shoe off into the cupboard under the stairs, attempting to hang up my duffle coat... And failing. I left it sat inside the cupboard... On my shoes.

"Has he been taking the mickey out of your new haircut?"

"No, he's got chicken po... Heeeyy... What do you mean? What's up with me haircut?" I looked in the mirror on the wall over the fire for reassurance.

"Chicken Pox... Ooh nasty." dad finally closed the door and returned to the lounge.

"Haircut, what's up with it??"

"Nothing, it looks lovely son, must of used a big bowl, though... Ha ha."

"Leave me hair alone, I'm growing a Georgie Best!"

"A whole Georgie Best... On your head? You will look strange!" I stared at him with utter contempt. "Okay, touchy. Why are you in a bad mood just because 'Napoleon Evil-heart' has got the chicken pox? You should be feeling sorry for the chicken pox!!" he always laughed at his own jokes, and today was no different as he put my friend down.

"No one to play wiv, hav I? I slumped onto the chair, hands in pockets.

"We bought you Trumper, didn't we, go throw a stick for him... Or go find yourself a girlfriend!"

I glanced up and sent him a dirty look, Trumper sat, just looking at me, happy to be in my company, whatever my mood. I looked down at my furry pal and stroked him between his ears, his tail lashed around a little in gratitude.

"What sort of dog is he, Dad?

"What... Errr, well... He's got parts of 27 different type's dog breeds in him son... Oh, and he's also part unmade bed... Ha ha... He's what you call a Moss Side Terrier." he dropped down onto his seat, pulling the newspaper out from beneath him afterwards.

"Stew's Dad said he looked like a big poo from the Bommimable Snowman's bum... With legs!" I scratched behind his ear, a leg began to kick uncontrollably.

My dad burst out laughing, again I just stared at him, and not believing this description of my dog was in any way hilarious.

"Snot funny, he's lovely aren't you Trumps?" he licked my hand in agreement.

"Hey, Stew's dad has only gone and white washed him, Dad! Stew waved at me from his bedroom while I was talking to his Dad, he's been painted white, and he looked like a ghost!"

"That's not white wash, you numpty, its calamine lotion!"

"White wash... 'copper mine lowshun'... Whatever it is... He's still not playing out." real sadness in my answer.

"Well, he'll be fine in a week, or so... " my dad was attempting to straighten the newspaper out, mum liked to have a read later on in the evening.

"A week!!!! You are joking! Oh my God, I'll have to play football with Digger, and he wears clogs, it always end up with me bruised and the ball popped! You're gonna have to play with me?"

"Me?... Not now? My knees are shot! Tell you what, we can play hide and seek!" he tried to make it sound as enticing as possible.

"No chance, last time we played, I hid in the coal bunker... Annnd... you know there's spiders in there, big 'uns too!" I held my hands apart about 18 inches to indicate the enormity of the arachnids. "Two hours I was hid... And I only came in when mum shouted me for bed. Where were you? YOU... " I pointed for emphasis, "... Had gone to the Lightbowne... You never even looked for me!!!!" my disgust was tangible... I folded my arms aggressively, and stared.

"I did, you're just too good, I tell you, if England had a 'hide and seek' World Cup side, you would be the captain... I looked everywhere for you... I even looked in the pub!" he explained lyrically.

"Well, that's true... I am very good at it, but that's not the point! I'm sure you just wanted a pint, then to top it all, mum went mental at me, just cost of a little coal dust on me clothes!"

"I know what we can do then!!!! We can play who can pull the ugliest face... " before I even had the chance to blink, never mind find a match winning gurn, he pointed at me "You win!!!" he burst out laughing again.

"Dad, I'm fed up... Stoppit!"

He dropped to his knees, opened his arms and began swaying slightly.

"Ding, ding... Round one... "

I jumped from the chair, and mirrored his stance, me standing, him kneeling.

"Wrestling... Right, I'm Mick McManus... Ha ha... Come on Trumpster, it's us against him... " I screamed.

I lunged into my Dad's arms, put his neck in the usually fatal, death lock, but he didn't seem to notice, he just lifted me in one quick surge... Then let me drop... Catching me just before I hit the floor.

"AHHHHH... Come on Trumper... Ahhh... Trumper... Attack... Stop wagging your flippin tail... You stupid dog," Trumper just ran in circles around our entwined bodies, like Indians around a surrounded Wagon Train "get him... No... Don't lick him... Ha ha... He's not going to give in like that... Bite his nose!"

Dad was lying on me now, squeezing me down with his weight. His nose in no danger, as Trumper looked on now.

"Ahhhh, Dad, I've got cramp... Ahhhhh... Let me out... Me leg... Ahhhhhh."

171

I pulled free and dragged myself, left leg ramrod stiff. I gripped and rubbed the calf as I edged towards the kitchen. Dad staring at me consternation.

"Where you going?"

"Ahhhhh… Put me leg on the cold lino, it cures it… " my face contorted in pain.

I lay my left calf on the linoleum. Release!

"Ooooh, that's better… " my leg relaxed, so did my features as the pain ebbed easily into the kitchen flooring.

"… And the winner is… Dad… Hoorah!" Dad cried out.

I whizzed round to see my father doing a celebratory dance, arms aloft, acknowledging the 'crowd!'

"No, I DON'T… FINK… SO, it was a draw."

"Trumper was referee, bark if I won." said Dad staring at Trumps.

Silence, dad turned slowly as I began to speak.

"There! Ha ha… Dad, he didn't bar… "

"Biscuits!!!" Dad cried out, looking at me now and not my dog.

"WOOOOOF" Trumper erupted from behind him.

Dad smiled, and his arms reached for the ceiling again.

"NOOOOOOoooo… That's cheating… Put your arms down. It's a draw… Trumper!!!!! How could you?… Dad… Stop dancing… Ha ha… And you stop wagging your flipping tail in my face, Trumper. I was robbed… DAAAAAD!!

172

## Baby Makes Three

"… All I'm saying is a baby should be taught tricks as soon as possible." I argued from the comfort of the rug, my head resting on Trumper's hind quarters.

"And all I am saying is, Brian, you are not allowed to put a four month old baby's head in Trumper's mouth like the man did on the telly, in the circus, at Xmas. What do you the think Sue would say? We look after her beautiful new baby daughter for the morning and she ends up with teeth marks on her head!!!!" she looked at me as if I had lost my mind.

"It'll only for a second… He's not gonna bite her, is he?… Let me just get a photograph… Then you can pull her away!"

"Oh, so not only endanger her life… We get some evidence of the fact… Seriously Brian? I know, why not sell the pictures to the News of the World too?" her head was shaking in dismay.

"Oooooh… Do you think we could make some money?" my eyes had opened to the size of saucers, in my head I had begun spending the rewards.

"I despair Brian, I really do, first you want to attach string to her arms and dance her like a puppet… Now you want to have her part of your lion taming act… For goodness sakes, you don't do that with little babies." she huffed and lifted baby Julie high, jiggling her slightly and continuing her baby talk to her.

"Do we, we don't do that, you're too beautiful for that sort of thing." she dropped her face to her near her mouth then blew a

173

raspberry on to her cherubic cheek, the vibrations caused a noise that made Julie giggle.

"Dad calls that a belly trump when he does it on my stomach... It makes me laugh as well... Why does trumping noises make everybody laugh, mum?"

"Well they don't make me laugh... Especially when your dad does them freestyle!" she said emphatically.

"What's freestyle?"

"It's when he just trumps, anywhere, with anyone, it's disgusting... Can we change the subject, please?"

"Dad says everybody trumps... Even the Queen!"

"Well... I don't... Subject closed, okay? Isn't it little girl...?" she wobbled Julie again, she answered mum with a toothless laugh.

"Never... You never trump?... Wonder why, cost I trump all the time... Dad says the more veg I eat... The bigger my trumps... And you eat loads of veg."

"Brian... Please... Two ladies like me and Julie, do not want to talk about bodily functions... Do we, Julie, do we? We want to talk about kissing cheeks... About... Pretty dresses... About little patent leather, shiny shoes... Lovely little bows for your hair."

"That's why women have never invented anything... They're too busy being soppy... One last thing mum, promise." I begged.

"What?" she stopped playing with the baby and stared at me and waited for my statement in trepidation.

"Dad says you can light your trumps... And in the dark... " mum tried to interrupt me.

"Brian Hamblett Junior, I cannot believe you think... " she failed.

"... They explode like the Saturn rockets on Apollo 11!!!" I smiled my broadest, cheekiest grin.

"... That this is an appropriate conversation to be having with two ladies!!!"""

"Sorry... But it would be funny... Booooom... He he." I lay on my back and lifted my legs back with my hands to emphasise the word boom.

"Have you finally finished?"

"Yeah, i suppose so. Can I put her in net and take shots at her, mum?" pointing at the radiogram, the legs were being the imaginary goalposts...

"No... Here, give me the camera... I'll take a picture of you with Julie on your knee."

"What? I don't wanna picture of me with a baby... Why would I?" I backed away slowly.

"Pass me the camera and sit here." I reluctantly passed her the small, black plastic camera. She motioned me to her side. "... And stop with the face like Piffy!"

"It's a baby... Can I look like I'm gonna put her head in my mouth?"

"Yes... Hurry up." I raced to her side, held out my hands and grabbed poor Julie under her arms.

"Ooooh, she heavy... And dead warm too!"

"Shush... Put your head at the side of hers... Smile."

"Should I look like I'm biting her ear off?" I opened my mouth, revealing my choppers.

"Okay... Let's see your best monster face... Growl... Grrrr" she laughed as I did my gruesome, Hammer House of Horror look, then she pretended to take a snap. "Now... Can I get a big smiley one of you to show her you really love her."

"Hey... I don't love her, like her, maybe... A bit... She's a girl, mum!!"

"... And smile... Smile... Cheese Brian... That's it... Let me take another in case you've got your eyes closed. Julie... Juuuulieeeee... " she snapped away like David Bailey.

175

"Mum… Mum… I don't want this anymore… I think she wants you."

"Do you love your cousin Brian, Julie?" she asked my little cousin.

"Mum… Stoppit… She needs you… Here… " I lifted her from my knee.

"Don't you want to give her a cuddle, Bri?" she smiled, teasing me.

"Nope… I don't think I'd cuddle anything that smells like poo!

"Oh no… Have you pooped little girl?" mum lay the camera down and approached.

"Either she has or I have!" I looked down at my grey shorts as mum lifted her away from me.

"I think you're a little old for that… Don't you Brian?" she tutted, she put Julie over her shoulder and took a small whiff of her nappy… Pulling away rather quickly.

"Well, you say that, but do you remember when I had the runs? It just came gushing out on its own… Right down me… " mum stopped me mid flow.

"Enough… Go, and take Trumper with you, he needs a walk, go on, put your coat on and let me and Julie have some girlie time… Yes… Should we… Babababa… Do you need a new nappy… A ba… A ba?" turning her attention from me to the smelly bundle in her arms.

"I'm going… " I slipped into my wayfarer shoes, "… but she'll grow up stupid, you know? She'll be talking like an idiot… Can you pass the… Aba aba… Aba… Goo goo… Salt please… Hello… My name is Ju… Ju… Ju… Goo goo… Lie… He he. Just talk normal to her, like I do with Trumper… " I made my way towards the door, knowing I was pushing her buttons.

"Get out... You don't know anything about babies... Does he gorgeous?" she lay her gently on her back and started to unbutton her baby grow.

"Come on Trumper... I opened the glass partition door that let you get to the front door. "Mum... Keep your matches handy... Just in case she trumps... He he!"

"Get out you heathen... " I kept on laughing as I stepped down into Lakin Street. Trumper loped out reluctantly... As I pulled the door closed mum got the last word. "... You don't take after me... I know that for sure... And, I'll be speaking with your father tonight... " there was a loud slam as I yanked it shut... The glass jangled loosely in the frame.

"Now there's a picture the News of the World would pay good money for, hey Trumps?" I skipped alongside my dog, heading off to the swingy, laughing out loud at the thought of the headline on Sunday, 'FIRST BABY LIFTS OFF FOR THE MOON!'

# CRIME AND PUNISHMENT

Grant 'Digger' Dalton was sat next to me on the garden wall outside a house in Douglas St and we both watched as the car drove onto Brendon Avenue then turned left onto Lakin Street. It pulled up almost immediately... Now this was a form of high entertainment in them days, pre X-Box, pre-PlayStation or even pre indoor toilets for some of us, you see we really didn't see many cars in 1968, and certainly not parking on Lakin Street in North East Manchester.

Drawn, we got up and wandered towards the shiny, black vehicle like we were approaching an alien spacecraft, wary but intrigued.

Now Digger was a unique chap... He was renowned to catching then eating Daddy Long legs. I am sure he only did this to shock us, and believe me, it always did... He would also dig up worms and we would watch in bemusement from a distance as he conversed with them like Dr, Doolittle. He loved talking to many things that most people would regard as limited in conversation, pencils, toy soldiers, crayons and keys. He really was the funniest little boy around, and just to top things off his feet were also constantly encased in wooden clogs and he sounded like a little pony walking alongside you... But you really could not help but love him?

The driver's door opened and a middle-aged man leapt out, he wore a white shirt with a sweat stain on his lower back and black creased trousers. He slammed the door shut and raced round to the passenger side and pulled that door open with a loud creaking noise from the hinge.

An elderly woman, with grey-blue hair and a camel coloured coat emerged slowly, I recognised her as one of my mates, Stews, neighbours who lived at number 34, she slid her legs sideways and let her feet touch the floor before she accepted the man's hand and was pulled up and out gently, she straightened up in slow motion then once she had got her bearings she approached her front door and stopped, looking down she let her hand fish inside a dark brown, leather handbag and it reappeared with a set of keys held between her index and forefinger, she smiled like she had won a prize in a fairground lucky dip. She turned and opened the front door to the house and walked in, the guy was holding two suitcases that he had retrieved from the boot and looked impatient as he followed her inside... He looked like he was liable to walk over her, this was a man in a hurry.

We had now crossed Brendon Avenue and we were stood by the car, both with our hands pushed deeply into our shorts pockets. No words had been spoken yet and we just stared.

The passenger door was still open and Digger sidled down the side of the car and popped his inquisitive head in, and immediately pulled it out and faced me... A mad smile spread across his face.

"Hey Hammy, the keys are still in!" he exclaimed.

"So... ... ?!" I asked as he stood smiling with a manic grin on his face.

Before I could say another word he dived across the leather seat and all I could see was his spindly legs and on the end of those linguine thin limbs were the enormous wooden and leather clogs.

"Whatcha doing?" I screamed, looking over my shoulder through the front door where the driver and his passenger had evaporated just moments before.

179

Digger slid out, put his face up against mine and screamed quietly, the words didn't sink in immediately, I had a moment to think, 'oh, Digger, you haven't cleaned your teeth this morning!' Then the words arrived...like a steam hammer!

"Gottem, run!!!" as he ran he held up one arm and jangled his ill-gotten gains.

I looked around, Digger had ducked under my arm that held the door ajar and raced the few yards to the corner of the street and like David Nixon... Disappeared!

"Got what?" I stood alone with my question, hand still leaning against the car.

Something in my brain slowly told me that he had stolen the man's keys, I decided it was not something I was about to take the blame for. I flew. I passed Stew's house a few doors down at about 67 mph. Crossed over to my side of the road, not looking for moving traffic, no park cars to camouflage me... Just a chubby boy running a personal best 200 metres, home.

As an escapee, I was rubbish... I had ran in a slight diagonal as far from the car as physically possible, but was in plain sight to anyone exiting the old woman's house. Digger had run ten feet and was out of sight! Even though his clogs were clip clopping down Douglas Street ginnel, anyone hearing it would think it was just an escaped donkey.

My front door was just inches away when I heard the call.

"Hey, stop!" Came the distant shout to my rear.

I just ignored its plea and pushed that door open, slammed it shut even faster, put the latch on, and then walked nonchalantly through the living room. My mother was brushing my dog, Trumper.

"Hello mum, I'm going to play in my room... See ya!!"

"Don't you want to play with Trumper?"

"Mum, I want to be alone!"

"Okay Greta Garbage... "

At that very moment there was a banging on the door, an urgent banging. I ran out of the living room and through the kitchen, pulled the wooden door hiding the staircase and ran upstairs taking two stairs per stride, I opened my bedroom door and closed it in one sweeping movement, rolled under the bed. Then finally remembered to breathe.

I had been there only one minute when the door opened and my mother's legs appeared, crossed the room and sat on my bed.

"Okay, what's going on Brian?" the voice came from above, calm yet insistent.

"It's wasn't me, it was Digger"

"What's he done?" same calm timbre.

"I think he's nicked keys from a man's car!"

"Brian, the man needs to drive back to London, where are the keys?" even more insistent, yet no threat, God she must of worked for the Nazi interrogators in the war!!!

"Diggers gottem… He's probably having a chat with them in his front room!" she'd broke me with her calm loving, caring, understanding tone, damn that woman!

Her legs stood.

"Right, out from under there, let's go to Grant's house."

I rolled out from beneath my bed, and followed her downstairs like a condemned prisoner walking the Green Mile.

A very jittery and nervous man was stood at our front door.

"Has your lad got the keys?"

"No, but we think we know where they are"

Mum locked the front door quietly, Dad was in bed after a few nights away driving his HGV round Scotland.

We walked up Lakin, over Brendon and into Douglas Street. At no. 11 my mum stopped and knocked on the door. Beatie Dalton, Digger's mum answered, she was not as calm and collected as my mum in a situation like this.

"Hello" she looked at all our faced then said "what's he bleeding done now?"

"It seems the boys have taken this man's keys from his car and he needs them to get home" explained mum

"Grant, get here you little sh*t" she screamed this at the top of her voice, didn't take her eyes off the three of us.

Beatie had a mild form of Tourette's I suspect, and would lace her sentences with Anglo Saxon basics without even realising.

"Where's the man's pi**ing keys, Grant?" she asked, as Digger's face appeared from behind her.

"I dropped them down the grid over there" he said pointing at the drain outside number 3 Douglas.

The man's shoulders slumped.

"You little s*it!!" Beattie swung and missed at his head.

"What am I going to do?" the man whined "I really need to get back to London "

My mother told him to calm down.

"I'll get my husband"

"No Mum, don't tell Dad, please, he'll kill me" I implored.

She ignored my begging and dragged me home, my feet struggling to keep up as we made our way back down Lakin.

To say my 6' 2" father was displeased to be roused from his sleep would not really do justice to his mood. He stared at me as he pulled on his jeans, he then glared at me as his head popped through his jumper. But still no words. That really was not a good sign.

We all walked to his lorry parked on Rudd Street, he opened his cab door and pulled out a long metal bar, and we marched, like dead men walking, all in silence, a preacher reading from the bible would not have looked out of place.

Dad levered open the drain cover with the metal bar, sweating, he pulled the heavy cover clear and with a deep clunk dropped it on the pavement. He then lay on the tarmac of the road and plunged his hand deep into the incredibly murky liquid that lay beneath. I watched his face, lay sideways on the stoned road surface, as he pulled a face like a man having his first prostate examination…from a doctor with Elephantitis of the fingers!

Then as quick as a flash his arm flew out, like a trout tickler with a bite, but in my dad's hand was not a rainbowed fresh water fish, but a set of keys, dripping, and with soggy rotting leaves attached. We got what was the nearest to a smile since he had been dragged from his bed.

"Thank God" said the man

"You, you little b\*\*tard, in that house" said Beattie menacingly to Digger… He ran off in the opposite direction, heading to Holland to claim sanctuary… Where he would blend in with his clipppity clop clogs.

I looked at my dad from behind my mother.

Then he finally spoke…

"You, my son, are going to the police station"

" But dad, I didn't do anyfink, honest "

"Cop Shop, Brian, as soon as I am washed"

The tears and begging to my mother continued all the way home, but she was unable to persuade him otherwise. This boy was about to be given the shock of his very young life.

Dad was ahead of us and reached home before me and Mum. By the time we arrived he was drying his arm, apparently washed and clean.

"Put his coat on, Marie" he said as he pulled a clean t-shirt over his head.

My mum looked at him and then opened the door under the stairs, brought out my black duffle coat, she knelt down and slowly did up the horn toggles, looking me in the eye and whispering…

"It'll be fine Bri, let your dad take you, you'll be okay"

Dad, stood by the front door, poker faced, his hand extended. I reached up and felt a stronger grip than normal, and off we went.

Onto Rudd, right on Lightbowne, past Steptoe's, the barber, across to Dave's the Newsagent, then straight down toward North Road. Old houses on both sides, Victorian homes that had outlived their use. I looked up at this giant of a man.

"I really didn't do anything Dad"

His response shocked me to the core, the man I loved, my hero, the man I aspired to be, smacked me so hard on my buttocks I didn't even react, so shocked he was even capable of this, I felt no pain. This was sixties 'shock and awe,' the second whack sorted the shock thing out, I wailed.

"I'm sorry dad, I didn't do anyfink… Honest!!"

Another whack, my brain screamed at me to shut up. My silence brought an end to the corporal punishment, so I thought to myself, no more words… No more pain.

The journey down Lightbowne was swift, my father walking faster than my little legs could manage. Tripping and having to be brought upright by my Dads strong arm. We reached the high wooden fences at the bottom of Lightbowne, the large advertisement poster for cigarettes that told me we were coming onto Thorpe Road, loomed high and large ahead.

We carried on in silence, at this uncomfortable pace for ten more minutes and then I spotted the blue lamp outside the Police Station, and I gulped, he was actually going through with it!

Dad pushed open the door, and shoved me into the small space before the desk.

A uniformed policeman, balding and fat with a Bobby Charlton comb over, stood with cup and tea towel in hand. He leaned over the front desk slightly so he could observe me, he then looked back at his cup and finished drying. He placed the cup next to three others and turned back to us.

"Hello, hello, hello, what have we here?" he asked in a stentorian tone.

"My son, it turns out, is a thief, he has stolen some keys from a car!" Dad said with disgust and shame.

I felt the need to interrupt.

"Actually Dad, I didn't, Digger took 'em... I"

"He's a liar too, is he?" said the bobby, interrupting my defence.

"I'm not mister! Honest" I said.

"... And argumentative!" he smirked at dad.

I looked at dad, with my eyebrows raised, looking for some back up. Nothing!

"Son, I find you guilty, you are hereby sentenced to 30 minutes in her Majesty's jail, Newton Heath!"

I looked at Dad, he stared at the chunky copper, and the rotund bobby smiled down at me...

"Come with me son" he lifted the wooden bridge that separated us from him, his sweaty, hairy hand grabbed mine. I stared over my shoulder at my disappearing father, his eyes took on that Botox look, 40 years before it was fashionable, mouth agape.

I was dragged down a corridor, the further into the building we went, the cooler it became, one hand reached back to where my dad was stood, the other was being pulled by the long arm of the law.

"Dad... Dad... Daddddddddd!!!!!!"

"Come on son, do your porridge quietly like a man" he demanded.

"But I ain't done anyfink mister, dadddddddd!!!" I squealed.

"Guilty. Half hour of hard labour" he insisted.

"You can't put me in jail... I haven't been to court... I haven't had a lawyer!"

"Well you are a right little Perry Mason, aren't you? Listen... I am Judge, Jury and executioner in this station son, I have found you guilty... Deal with it... The heavy door slammed shut with a bang. A metal letterbox slid to one side and his eyes appeared.

"I don't think that man is my real dad, I think I may have been kidnapped me from the gypsy's!"

"Stolen 'from' the gypsy's, that's a new one... 29 minutes and you'll be free, sit down and think about what you have done and if you ever want to be in one of these again!!" the policeman's voice echoing round my cell through the small gap in the door... Then with a metallic clang it slid shut.

He returned to my father who stood in shock.

"Right matey, a nice brew of Rosie Lee, let your boy stew on his balls up"

It was a good 15 seconds before the real screaming began, begging for freedom, imploring my father to get me out of there. The sobbing was next, real, difficult to breathe, sobbing... Words coming out between the blubbering Snot dangling from my nose like a glistening rope.

"Dad, I'm sorry. Dad, don't you love me?... Dad, I think I'm going to be sick... "

"Leave him, enjoy your brew, it will do him the world of good". Insisted the cop.

When I was released, I was a broken boy. Face sodden with tears, heartbroken that it had come to this. I walked with head bowed from behind the desk.

"Right son, if I see you again, I will make sure you are locked up for a very, very long time!"

I nodded, there was no fight left.

We walked out of the station, the door swung to with a bang. My dad's big hands came down slowly and with all that anger dissipated, he lifted me into his big chest, both arms enveloping me, the hug was firm and insistent, it spoke volumes... It said that he forgave me... And it asked if I could forgive him.

"I love you Dad, and I'll be a good boy forever. Promise."

"You bloody better Brian, I can't go through that again... "

A call at Dave's newsagent shop for a Matchbox version of red Ferrari made us both feel a lot better.

Later when I was allowed out, the first person I saw was Digger, sat on his doorstep, big grin on his face, a jam butty half eaten in his hands and Tej, his black, mongrel dog, lay like a big black turd, curled round at his feet.

"Hammmmmmmeeeee!!!"... And the biggest, triumphant laugh.

"I could strangle you... You insect eating, wooden footed bugger... Cheerfully strangle you, I've been locked in prison... And my bums killing me!."

"I think you better explain that last statement, Hammy, because it could be taken out of context!!

## The Last Goodnight

**(A tribute to my father who sadly passed away the previous night)**

"Daadddd... Dadddd." I called as I heard him climb the stairs, probably nipping to the loo. My door creaked open slowly, the big smiling face of my lovely father appeared in instalments, bit by bit

"Hey, you should be asleep, Bri." he whispered

"I had a nightmare Dad."

"A nightmare, eek!! Sounds scary... Monsters, ghosts or was you running around school with no clothes on... Waving your arms above your head?" he was laughing, but still keeping his voice low.

"Noooooo Dad, I dreamt you weren't coming home again!" there was a wavering tremble in my voice.

"Why, in high heavens, would I not be here, Bri? Good food, you two and your beautiful Mum, I'd have to be mad not to be the happiest man alive... I'm going nowhere!"

"But I dreamt it, Dad... I kept looking for you, I looked everywhere, but I couldn't find you!"

"Brian Hamblett Junior, you have been looking in all the wrong places, son." he stepped inside my room now, he was a dark silhouette now, the landing light shining behind his head like a halo.

"Well, I know that don't I... You've disappeared... An' I can't find you! If I knew where you was... It wouldn't be a nightmare... It would be a dream!" I tutted.

"Well, for a start, calm down... Right, this is easy, because you are me!"

"Now you're being sarcarsick... I hate that." I started to turn in my bed, away from his ethereal shape.

"Hey... I'm not, you are actually 49% me, 51% your mum, that's how you were made in your mum's belly. It's scientific fact! So, if you ever feel I am just too far away, all you have to do is close your eyes, breathe slowly in and even slower out, allow yourself to hear your heartbeat, and when you're nice and relaxed, that's when you'll hear me, you'll feel that 49% of you that is me. That will be better than me being by your side, son... I'll be right inside, you will calm down and know I am never further than 2 minutes away, hugging you from the inside out... That's what I do with my mum, and she passed away before you were born!" his words were softer as he spoke of his mother.

"I know, I never met her, do you miss her, Dad?" I'd sat up on my elbows now, trying without success to see his expression in the dark.

"Of course, but sometimes, when I am alone, and you two aren't causing mayhem, I may be lay on the sofa, and just I just allow myself to drift gently back to the good old days when I was young, and eventually, it's like she's there, and I  smile... They were good days."

"Well... What if you die, Dad!" I asked, anxiety washing over me.

"Blimey... Well, If I die, Bri, I will just be in another place... A place that is only a cigarette skin's width away, almost so close you can see me, and in that place... I will be building the best home, just preparing for when it's everybody else's turn to come across... There'll be a bath, 3 bedrooms, colour telly... "

"Colour telly. No way!!!!" I interrupted.

"Of course Bri, its Heaven… It's all we will want it to be."

"But this is all I want it to be Dad… Why do we all have to die?"

"So people can grow, learn, have children, so they, in turn, can grow and learn… "

"Spose, if they didn't… I wouldn't be here!?"

"Exactly… We all get a turn. So don't be scared. Don't worry about it. But always make the best of your turn… And anyway… I'm going nowhere for a long, long time!"

"Promise Dad?" I asked.

"I promise… When it's my time, son, I will make sure you have enough wonderful memories of me in your memory bank to keep you happy forever!" he stepped back.

"Well, think I can sleep now Dad."

"Good, because I've needed to pee for ages!! But if you ever need me Bri, and I mean ever, just look inside… There I am!"

"Okay, Dad, you can go now… "

"Bye son." he turned away and I saw him as the light shone on his face, a warm light for this gentleman… An image burnt onto my retina… I closed my eyes so I could bank it for future reference.

"Bye Dad." I said softly.

The door started slowly closing to… Light diminishing.

"Dad, don't forget… " I called before he left.

"What, son… ?" it was just his voice now and his shadow being cast large on my bedroom wall.

"I love you, and when I grow up… I want to be just like you"

"Ha ha… " behind the door he laughed that glorious, balmy, genuinely happy laugh, the one that made you feel that he was happy with every aspect of his life.

"I told you... You ARE me... And when you grow up... You must be better than me, Bri... Okay." the voice was insistent, but caring.

"Ha... Impossible Dad... You are the best... The very, very, very, very... In fact the bestest Dad in the world... He he."

"Goodnight Bri, goodnight Alan"... The door closed... And a light went out... Sadly, my life would be ever so slightly dimmer for his exit.

In the dark, I could hear his quiet, slightly out of tune whistle, a real comfort, he's still there I though, and the tune he whistled? 'Those were the days my Friend'... Oh, yes, they certainly were dad!

In memory of my wonderful father who sadly turned a light out for me last night, God bless you, you wonderful man... You fantastic father... You glorious husband and playground to your grandchildren... Friend of many, enemy of none. My hero. Everything I ever aspire to be...

BRIAN HAMBLETT Snr. (b. 26/2/1933 d. 9/12/13)

10 December 2013 at 15:27

9925984R00107

Printed in Great Britain
by Amazon.co.uk, Ltd.,
Marston Gate.